Living God's Plan

for my life

DICK MERKLE

Auctorem House
276 5th Ave, Ste 704-2591
New York, NY 10001
www.auctoremhouse.com
1.888.332.7718

Introduction

- God created me in the year 1941.
- He called me to be a coach and a high school teacher.
- His plan for me was, to live in Beaverton, MI where:
- I would teach Biology for 34 years
- I would coach 67 different athletic teams
- I would mow 87 different lawns, mainly for widow ladies and the elderly
- I would give His commencement address in 1984 to the Beaverton graduates
- I would teach a Sunday school class and become a lay speaker in the Beaverton United Methodist Church
- God has also taught me five new parables concerning Scriptures from His Word.

God has a life plan for all people, whether we are aware of it or not. I was unaware of following the plan God had for me, until I began reading the Bible and until I became a Christian. Then as I reflected on my life, I could see how my life unfolded, as if on a plan, **God's plan**. I hope, as others read this book, they will become aware of the plan God has for them. Included in God's plan for me was to read and study the Bible, regularly, so that He could teach me, via His Holy Spirit, the meanings of His Word, especially, the five new parables He taught me. They will be written, later, in this book.

Foreward

I started my Bible reading on a very low level, as I would 'force myself' to read for a whole sum of only one chapter a night. This lasted for a few weeks, then I decided to read for a time of ten minutes in whatever Book of the Bible that I was reading. I started in Matthew and then progressed, in order, reading through the whole New Testament. As I continued reading I increased my reading to two chapters per night, then five chapters per night. As I continued to read, the Bible actually became interesting to me, and I could hardly wait until the next night, so that I could read the Bible again. As I continued to progress in my reading time, I added five chapters of the Psalms to my reading schedule along with the five chapters of the Old Testament. I now, had a reading schedule that included <u>15 chapters each time/day</u>:

   5 chapters from the Old Testament, 5 chapters of the Psalms or 5 chapters from the book of Proverbs, along with 5 chapters from the New Testament.

   This regiment of reading the Bible, once I reached a minimum of 15 chapters per day, went on for a period of at least 7 ½ years. No matter where I was or what I was doing, I always read 15 chapters in the Bible every day. I also switched to early mornings, so that I started my day with God's Word. I also did other readings of books from different Christian writers. The book that probably had the most profound effect on me was Charles Colson's book, "Born Again". While reading this book the Holy Spirit finally penetrated my heart and convinced me that I had to ask Jesus to be my Savior. After Jesus came into my life and I became a 'born again' Christian, Bible reading, really came alive to me as The Holy Spirit revealed to me many new understandings about the Scripture, in ways that I had never before thought of, nor heard anyone else explain them in such a way. **I Corinthians Chapter 2, Verses 6–16** tell us that no one can understand the thoughts of God, unless The Holy Spirit reveals them to us.

1

This book is my attempt at writing the things that I think, God has specifically called me to do and where I was to live and to write down the revelations given to me by The Holy Spirit. I call these understandings 'new revelations' or 'modern day parables'. These revelations are in no way an exhaustive nor a complete explanation of the teachings in The Bible, but only the revelations of some of the Scriptures given to me in ways I could understand and only about those Scriptures that God was ready to reveal to me. As you read through the various 'parables' you may notice that some of the ideas may be repeated, but you should also notice that the similar ideas are with a different set of Scripture verses. To the best of my recollection I tried to put the ideas down as the Holy Spirit revealed them to me.

Some of these ideas came to me while mowing lawns; while working in the garden; while driving the car and many of these revelations came in the middle of the night. Frequently, I would wake up at 1a.m., 2a.m., or 3a.m. with thoughts of Scripture verses in my mind. If I would lay awake for more than 15 minutes, I used that as a signal to get up, find that Scripture in the Bible and begin reading. Every time that I responded to this 'call', God was faithful and would reveal to me, some new understanding about that Scripture. The words of the Scripture literally seemed to come alive. I remember thinking "WOW! So that is what this Scripture means". These revelations almost always applied to some part of, or something in my life, to which I could relate.

As stated in the introduction, I am a Biology teacher, so God would often show me how the Scripture relates to living things that He created: flowering plants, ripening fruit, potato hills, even our stomach and food. The Biology II class that I taught at Beaverton, was divided into two semester sections. During the fall term I taught a section on Zoology and dissection of animals. In the spring term of the same year, I then taught a section on Botany. In the class the students studied the basic plant parts, the cells that made up each plant part, different plant types, twig characteristics to use for tree identification and the processes of pollination; flower, fruit and seed development.

I had been reading the Bible for many years and had taken many notebooks full of notes before God gave me these parables as a way to gain a better understanding of His Word. He taught me in ways that I was familiar with, as a teacher of Biology, Botany & Driver's Education. These revelations tied together the ideas in God's Word with the ideas that I taught in my high school classes and in events in my everyday life.

Whether we know it or not God has a plan for the life of every person that He creates and that has been born. This book is my attempt to explain how I think that I am living God's plan for my life, including relating the modern day parables that He has revealed to me.

The following ideas are key events that have happened in my life and I believe that they were ordained by God. I will list each key event in short phrases then explain each, later.

[Commencement speech; whole world based on love; someday you will be a coach; fear of dying; moved to Michigan; met and married my wife; accepted teaching job at Beaverton Rural Schools; coached different sports; began Bible reading; mowed lawns for widows and retirees; modern day parables]

Perhaps the most meaningful way in which God revealed part of His plan for my life occurred through a dream. I had a dream that I was talking at some commencement service at the end of a school year. That is the next thing that I want to share with you readers.

2

Commencement Address
1984

Seniors and friends,

I would like to thank all of you for the opportunity of talking to you this evening. I consider this to be a distinct privilege and a great responsibility to share some ideas with you, tonight.

Last summer, I had an opportunity to hear a man by the name of Dr. George D. LeMoore, who is a professor at Iowa Wesleyan University, relate the shortest commencement address that he had ever heard. He said the address was this:

"**Socrates** said, 'heal thyself'; **Plato** said 'know thyself', **Jesus** says, 'give thyself.'" The speaker then sat down. Well, I would like to take a little longer, tonight.

Trying to come up with a topic that would be of interest to all people, here tonight, is an almost impossible task. Had it not been for an event that happened to me eight months ago, I would probably have declined the invitation to speak to you tonight. That event, gave me a topic that concerns all of us, whether we think about it, or not.

I have read of a man by the name of Peter, who was on trial because of some of the things he said and taught. One of the civil authorities stood up during the trial and said, "Fellow citizens! There are many groups and people, preaching ideas today, so it won't matter if we listen to this one. If he is teaching false ideas they will soon pass away and be forgotten, but, if he is telling the truth, we must not fail to listen."

I would like you to give me 10–12 minutes of your time, tonight, with those thoughts in mind. If what I have to say is false, you can soon forget what I'm going to tell you, but, if what I say is true, these could be the most important 12 minutes of your life.

One day in January, Regina Stocco and Sandy Rice came to me, between classes and asked me if I would be willing to give a talk at commencement, this year. I very willingly and excitedly said, "Sure, I'd be glad to. In fact, I knew that I was going to be asked."

During the night of 11/17/83, at 2:27 a.m., I awoke from a dream that had me standing, right here, talking to you people and it was at this commencement. I was talking to you about the need to do your homework and about the different types or ways of doing homework. I believe this dream was God's way of telling me that He wanted me to talk at this commencement and that I should be ready to say, yes, when asked.

Commencement means beginning. All of you know that is why we are here tonight, to honor the graduating seniors and recognize the beginning of their adult lives after high school. For those who are graduating from night school, tonight also marks a new beginning for you. You all, now have a high school diploma and we can only hope and pray that it will help new doors of opportunities to open for you.

For all of you that are graduating, tonight's ceremonies should give you some challenges and guidelines on how to pattern your life to make it rewarding and worthwhile, for you, and all others that you come in contact with.

Many of you graduates are ready to begin college in the fall; some of you may still be making plans to attend college; some of you may be ready to start a job; while others of you may still be looking for a job and probably a few of you, don't know what you are, going to do. Whatever you end up doing for your vocation, it's a sure 'bet', that you will all have similar goals. These goals will probably include such things as: owning your own home; having a family; having enough money to satisfy your needs and enough money to buy many things that you don't need, but, sure are nice to have. Other goals may be: becoming a successful doctor; or lawyer; or insurance man; a farmer; perhaps even a professional athlete; maybe even a teacher.

But you know what? This drive for money and success is not completely satisfying, by itself. There is more to life than all the things I just mentioned.

How many times have you heard it said, that money can't buy and doesn't buy happiness? Probably, we've all heard it, but we don't want to believe someone else. We want to find out for ourselves.

Most of us think how nice it would be if we won the million dollar lottery or were given a 'fat' multi-million dollar contract like Steve Young, from Brigham Young University, received from the USFL LA Express football team. At the time of his signing, he had not played one minute of professional football, but yet, he was given a contract that will be worth 40 million dollars. All he has to do is play football for 4 years and he will be paid a salary, over a period of 43 years, that will be worth 40 million dollars.

[*I'm just hoping that with my teaching salary, I'll be able to save 43 dollars in 40 years*]

By themselves, money and success are not bad. The Bible says that, "It is the love of money that is the root of all evil." If our 'aim in life' is to attain personal wealth and success, over all other things, then we are 'shooting' at the wrong target. The plans of even the wisest humans are all for naught, if they do not include God, nor make room for Him. If we ask God to help us develop our <u>aim in life</u>, He will give us <u>the proper target</u>, with success and money as fringe benefits.

Unless you are going to college, perhaps you, graduates, think that your homework is over. But I would like to suggest, that maybe only a few of you have begun the most important homework of your lives: that is, finding out Who or What God is and what He expects of each of you.

I hope that since all of you have successfully reached graduation tonight, you have learned that you should not 'turn yourself off' towards an idea, if you have never made an attempt to learn about it. When students come into my class at the beginning of the year and say, "I do not like Biology," I ask them how they can make such a judgment without even trying to learn Biology. I also say, "Tell me you hate Biology after you've taken the class for 10 weeks." Occasionally, I have one or two tell me that they still hate the class and want to get out. "Fine," I tell them, "at least you made an effort to learn and now you have some basis for your opinion."

I think we must do the same thing when it comes to forming and stating an opinion about God. Don't say that you hate God nor don't believe in Him, out of ignorance, due to a lack of study. As a mature person, make a concentrated effort to learn something about God before you try to form an opinion, pro or con.

I also tell my Biology students that it is more important to spend 10–20 minutes each day, studying each subject, to keep them fresh in your mind, rather than cramming for one hour, once a week, before a test. I think the same type of daily effort is necessary to learn about God.

I would like to challenge all of you, graduates and everyone here tonight, to begin doing your homework for God, if you haven't already started. Even though, this homework may be the most important of your life, it can also be the easiest.

Studying the Bible can be much easier than studying Biology. In Biology a person has to try to memorize all the new terms that are talked about, how to spell them, what do they mean and what do they do or look like. You really have to put your brain to work.

But, the Bible assures us, that if we let Him, the Holy Spirit will teach us all things concerning God. However much effort you put into your homework, that will be the extent of your learning about God, just as the extent of your homework or study in high school determined how much you learned in your 12 or 13 years of schooling you have now completed.

Why bother with this type of homework? I can almost hear some of your thoughts: who cares about all this religion 'jazz' and talk about God? Bear with me just a little while longer.

Every day, whether you want to admit it or not, we all acknowledge the existence of God and the life of Jesus even if we are not aware of it. Let me give you a few examples.

What is today's date, the date of your graduation? It is 6/01/84. What does the year 1984 imply? It means that it has been 1,984 years since the man named Jesus lived and died on earth. Every time we write the dates 1984, 85, 86 etc. we acknowledge the fact that God did live on earth for a period of time and we know how many years ago this event occurred. It is a fact of History.

Earlier tonight, we had an invocation. Why would we take time to offer a prayer to God, if He does not exist?

Your class motto definitely suggests some Bible teaching to me. The parts, 'today well lived' and 'every tomorrow a vision of hope,' remind me of the verse said by Jesus, "I have come that you may have life and have it more abundantly." Because He came, lived, died and arose again, we can have hope for many more tomorrows. Hope is actually a gift from God.

Twice during this school year, we had two, week-long vacations: Christmas and Easter. Both of these vacations exist because God exists. He was born to live on earth at Christmas and He died and arose from the dead at Easter.

Why would President Reagan be trying to get prayer back into schools and declared 5/03/1984 a National Day of Prayer, if there is no God?

We often hear of the moral majority. To me, this means that most people have a basic sense of right and wrong. This basic sense is innate in our character, because God created all of us and implanted this idea in our minds. Unfortunately, we let pressures of our society warp and bend this basic sense.

I read in a book titled, <u>Revolution Now</u> by Bill Bright, a statement related to the pressures in a society. He said that, "Individuals make up a society. Selfishness, prejudice, hate, greed and lust are all individual problems which become the problems of collective man and societies. Our problem is solved then, if the individual is changed."

How did society become a collection of individuals? Why is there no common bond to bring individuals together? The Bible states one reason [**Matthew 14:27**] "The Shepherd will be killed and the sheep will be scattered." That's what is wrong with our society, today. Our Shepherd was killed about 1,984 years ago and most of us have been wandering around like lost sheep, because of it.

Daj Hammerskjold, former Secretary General of the United Nations, made a statement that is also related to our mixed up society. He said, "I see no hope for world peace. We have tried so hard and failed so miserably. Unless the world has a <u>spiritual rebirth</u> within the next few years, civilization is dead."

Man's efforts at changing individuals and societies are only temporary. The Bible tells us that only Jesus, can change us, successfully. Jesus was the perfect human and He wants to help us pattern our lives after Him. So, when you use the expression, "Oh, it's only human nature," perhaps we should be referring to, the 'nature of the Perfect Human Jesus Christ' and not to the carnal nature of humans and therefore, set for ourselves, a higher goal of personal worth.

There is one more bit of evidence to prove God's existence in the world and it is probably the most important. It is evident in this gymnasium, tonight. All of you are here because you are an immediate family member, a relative or a friend of one of the graduating seniors. Each of you is here because of the love that you have for your particular graduate. All of us here, love someone and we probably love those people more than ourselves. This capacity to love others is also born into us and it was given to us and to mankind by God. The Bible, in many places, states that God is Love and the more we learn of God, the more we can learn to love others.

Parents, I suggest to you, that possibly the greatest graduation gift you could ever give to your son or daughter is your total love and give them a chance to learn, Who, God is. I can tell you and God will guarantee it, that, if you do help them learn to know God and Jesus before they go off to college or leave home, you will never have to worry about them. This doesn't mean that everything will be 'peaches and cream', that they will pass all of their classes, nor that they will never have any problems. But it does mean, that they will never do anything that will disgrace or dishonor you or themselves.

Is your homework really over? Thank you and may God bless all of you.

3

I would now like to continue with the other ways in which I think that I have been living God's plan for my life. I listed them earlier, at the end of chapter one.

**Whole world based on love

I was born in 1941. All of these ideas/events started when I was very young, back in the late 1940s or early 1950s, while I was in the 4th and 5th grades in elementary school. One day, while laying on the couch, because I had the mumps, I was listening to the radio. As one song was playing, the thought came to me, that, that song was about love. Shortly after that thought, a second thought came that many songs are about love, then the final and most profound thought came, that the whole world is based on love. After becoming a Christian and thinking back on that experience, I believe that those ideas were given to me by God and it was His way of first communicating with me, something about His Nature and Who He is. This idea is verified in the Scripture, **I John 4:8** *Whoever does not love does not know God, because **God is love**. As you read the remaining verses in Chapter 4, love is talked about 10 more times. Some are referring to God's love and the others tell of the love we should have for others.

**You will be a coach

The second event that happened at about the same time, had perhaps the most influence on my life. God called me to be a coach, during this same time frame. It happened in this way: I was standing in the gym, in Wilshire, Ohio, where I attended school, watching the varsity basketball coach who was shooting baskets for awhile, then he would go beyond half court, throw the ball up through the open steel rafters of the ceiling and have it come down, bounce on the floor and then bounce up towards the basketball rim. He would do this until he successfully made one basket, then he would quit for that day. While watching him one day the following thought passed through my mind: '**Someday you will be a coach**'. The thought wasn't that I wanted to be a coach, like Mr. Games, but that **I would be** a coach. At that time I did not think too much about this thought. I now believe that, that thought, was God's call for me, to fit into His plan for my life. As I grew older and got into high school I began reading many books from the library that were related to sports and this reading 'worked' into my mind the desire for sports and the desire to play sports while in high school. I played baseball and basketball each year. Even though I was not very tall nor was I blessed with great ability, I did have the desire to work hard and do the best that I could and I made each team that I 'tried out for'.

We moved to Michigan during my sophomore year, then moved to a different school at the beginning of my junior year. These moves affected my playing of sports. As a senior, in a new school, I only played basketball, but my 'love' for sports kept growing inside of me. I knew that I was not gifted enough to be a college player and the only way I could continue to be involved in sports was to become a coach. Even though I had this thought, I never believed that I would be able to go to college to study to be a coach, because I came from a 'farming family' and my dad never had much extra money and especially, not enough to send me to college. But, because of '<u>God's call</u>' on my life, He had '<u>His Plan</u>' already worked out for me, which led me into a teaching and coaching career.

Read the following Scripture verses that tell how God has a plan for all people.

Psalm 139:16b <u>*All the days ordained for me*</u> *were written in Your Book before one of them came to be.*

Job 14:5 *Man's days are determined; You have decreed <u>the number of his months</u> and have set limits he cannot exceed.*

Acts 17:26 *From one man, He made every nation of men, that they should inhabit the earth: and He determined <u>the times set for them and the exact places</u> where they should live.*

Ephesians 2:10 *For we are God's workmanship, created in Christ Jesus <u>to do good works</u>, which God prepared, in advance, for us to do.*

Ephesians 4:1 *As a prisoner for the Lord, I urge you <u>to live a life worthy of the calling</u> you have received.*

**Fear of dying

A third event that began in the early part of my life also had a major effect on me. I had a major fear of dying. This fear lasted for many years. This fear was manifested in two kinds of night dreams and even daydreams. These dreams all seemed to be of two similar kinds: I would visualize myself floating in some dark void or I was being chased by some dark animal. These dreams began when I was seven or eight years old and they persisted, off & on, until I was in my thirties. Perhaps this fear of dying developed in me, because I had a 3 years old brother die when I was only five years old. My brother's death may have played a role in the development of my fear of death.

The most common daydream was the one where I would be floating up in some dark void. I could visualize myself in a curled up fetal-type position. While in this position, I could also see myself looking down onto the place where I lived with my family. The scary thing about this vision was, that I could see various members of my family, going about their daily routines but none of them knew where I was nor even knew that I was not with them. These dreams occurred several times in a month for several years, until I was an adult.

The other type of dream that I often had, was that I was being chased by some type of dark carnivorous animal. The faster I tried to run, the slower it seemed that I was actually running and I could feel my legs getting heavier, thus causing me to slow down. Fortunately, before the animal ever caught me, I would wake up from the dreams.

God helped me get over this fear of death through another dream that He gave me. Romans 8:28 is a Scripture that tells us how God will, can and does help us: *"And we know that in all things, God works for the good of those who love Him, who have been called according to His purpose"*

In this dream I was being chased/followed, but not by some dark animal but by some black men. In this dream, I was walking by myself, in some large city and I thought it to be Lansing, Mi. As I was walking, I began to notice that the buildings were getting darker and darker, the farther I walked. I began thinking that I must be walking in a black neighborhood area. The other thing that bothered me, the buildings seemed to be getting closer to me as the street seemed to be getting narrower. As I continued walking, I began to hear foot steps behind me and when I turned to look, there were two black men following me. Their steps got louder as they got closer to me and the street was continuing to narrow. My fear became much greater and I began to hurry to the end of the street. During the last few minutes of this time, some of the words of the **23rd Psalm** began to 'run through' my mind; *"yea, though I walk through the valley of the shadow of death, I will fear no evil, for Thou art with me"*. As these words went through my mind I came to the end of this dark street and I recognized the name of the street on the signpost. I thought, 'I know where I am'. I turned and looked to the right and at the end of the street, that I recognized, I saw a bright light and I knew it was the 'Light of God'.

I have had no fear of dying, since that dream.

**Married Lois

Before becoming a senior, as I wrote earlier, we moved to Michigan. We first moved into the Quincy school district then after a year, we moved into the Union City school district. Sometime, during my sophomore year of high school, I had the thought that when the 'right' girl came along, who would become my wife, that somehow I would immediately know it. I did not do any random dating while in high school, in fact, I seldom thought about girls or going on dates. During my junior year, my dad took my brother and I and our church youth group to a church in Athens, MI for a combined fellowship meeting. At that meeting I saw a girl, Lois, who peeked my interest. We visited for a little while and then it was time to go home. For the next few weeks, I thought of Lois, quite often and finally got up enough nerve to call her to ask her for a date.

During this time, Lois and I continued to date, even after her graduation while she attended college. I worked for one year in a small machine shop and was able to save half of the money to start one year of college at Michigan State University and my dad was able to give me enough money for the other half. However, after one year I had to drop out of college and take a job, in order to make and save money for the remainder of my college studies. As Lois and I continued to date we began to think about getting married and I told her that she would need to continue to work to help make money for us, so that I could finish my college. She agreed. We got married in June of 1962.

5

**Move to Beaverton

After finishing college I had a Bachelor's degree, with majors in both Science and in Physical Education. Lois and I began to look for a teaching/coaching job to start my career. We knew that we had to send out resume letters [*as they were called at that time*] to various schools, but we did not know where we wanted to send them. So we came up with an unusual idea. We sat down at our kitchen table and laid an open Michigan map out in front of us. I told Lois that I was going to close my eyes and then place the point of my finger on the map and she was to write down the name of the closest town near my finger. We did this for 15 towns and sent letters to each of the high schools in those towns. We heard back from only 3 schools; Bellaire, Evart & Beaverton. Beaverton High School was the only school that had a Biology teaching assignment available, so that is the school I chose. At the time, it seemed that I/we chose to go to Beaverton, not knowing that it was all in <u>God's Plan</u> for our lives. Reread the Scripture; **Acts 17:26** that I quoted earlier.

I started my teaching career at Beaverton in the last couple of weeks of December 1966. Beaverton was short of teachers at that time and the History teacher was teaching extra classes so that Biology could be taught. So when I was hired in, he was able to lessen his load and only teach the Social Studies classes, as I took over the Biology classes and some General Science classes that he had been teaching. The man that I replaced in the Biology classroom was also, the varsity basketball coach. I had no idea that they were wanting to get rid of him, at that time. As stated earlier he was one of the Social Studies teacher and he had agreed to teach the Biology classes to help out the school. The 'school rewarded him' by taking away his coaching assignment and giving it to me in 1968. Little did I know that a similar thing would happen to me, three years later.

Some of us teachers were sitting in the teacher's lounge, at lunch, when in walked this man who said, "Hi, my name is Larry Niederstadt, and I am the new varsity basketball coach". At the time of this writing, I have still not been told officially, 'by the school' why they took the job from me. **BUT!!**

Remember, that I told you, that way back in the 1950s, God told me that someday I would be a coach. He did not say what kind of a coach I would become. I actually had a good coaching career for 22 years. But, it did not start until I made peace with God, so that He could make peace in my heart towards the Beaverton School Board for taking away the varsity basketball coaching job from me. I actually coached JV Basketball, with Larry, as the varsity coach for several years. We became very good friends during our years while coaching together.

My whole coaching career consisted of 3 years helping out with varsity football, 21 years as head JV football coach, 9 years varsity baseball, 2 years JV baseball, 3 years as varsity boys basketball coach, 15 years JV boys basketball, 7 years JV girls basketball, 5 years girls JV volleyball, 3 years as girls varsity volleyball coach and finally 2 years as varsity boys golf coach. During my JV football coaching, the first two seasons the teams went undefeated, because of the God-given talent that the players had, then a few seasons later, the team had no wins. During my JV basketball coaching, we had one undefeated season and one season we had no wins. I found out that the longer you coach the more variety of successes and failures you will have.

**20-0 JV Basketball season

I would like to 'tell' a little of how an undefeated JV Basketball season came about. I had become a Christian prior to the season and was doing much Bible reading and praying. As the season progressed, the team built up more and more wins until they were 15-0. During this stretch we had defeated Evart, by only five points at our school. Evart had two tall players, a 6'6" center and a 6'3" forward. When the came time to go to Evart for our second game, I prayed to God on Sunday night and during the week, to give me some new ideas to help the team stay undefeated. I also prayed, help me, so that I don't cause the team to lose because of some coaching mistakes, I might make. He gave me two ideas that I had never used before. The first idea was to ask the varsity coach if we could use his tall center, 6'8", at the beginning of practices, that week, so the players could learn to defend a big man, both in front & behind; double team him. The coach agreed. The other idea I was given was to use a full-court press after every basket we, Beaverton, made and drop back to a half-court press on missed baskets. Both of these ideas proved valuable as we beat Evart, on their home court. On the opening tip we got control of the ball and went down and scored a lay-up basket for the first points of the game. On the proceeding in-bounds pass by Evart, our point guard stole the pass and made another lay-up to give Beaverton a 4-point lead with only 12 seconds gone off of the clock The team never let up the pressure and they went on to defeat Evart by 32 points and they were able to complete a perfect 20-0 season.

**Lawn mowing mission:

Another part of God's plan for me in Beaverton, was to become a lawn mower or as I thought later, He took me to Beaverton to become a "care-taker of God's green earth in Beaverton". When our twin boys were in the 7th grade of school, three widow ladies in our church asked Lois and I, if we would allow our boys to mow their lawns. We said, yes, we would give them permission and this was the beginning of my/our mowing for God by helping others. The first year the boys only had the three lawns to mow for the widow ladies. So I would take them to the lawns on Saturday and watch them mow and help them out, if they got too tired or hot. The next year, our number of lawns to mow, expanded to eight lawns. I bought a riding lawn mower for the boys so that they/ we could get all the lawns mowed, each week. Then the third year the number of lawn customers went up to fifteen. One night, in prayer, I told God that if He would give me the ability to buy a new, bigger, riding lawn mower I would put it to work for Him, by doing for others as His Word tells us to do. Well, He did and I/we mowed for others for the next forty years. Most of the time I had 22-25 lawns to mow, each week. My twin boys helped with the lawn mowing for the six years that they were in school. Most of the people that the boys and I helped were widow ladies, retired people or handicapped people. I did mow for a few neighbors and friends that we knew but, who did not fit the 'needed' category. Our pay started out by the three widow ladies agreeing to give each of my boys, $3.50 per hour. As new people asked us to mow their lawns, we told them that we would charge them $7.00 per hour, the same as the twins, were first paid. As I got new customers, I stayed with the same hourly wage after the boys left high school and no longer helped me. As the years increased and I continued mowing for the same people, they voluntarily gave me more money than I asked for. After thirty years of mowing the increase that people were giving me amounted to $15.00 per hour. Do for God and He will cause the increase.

I/we actually mowed eighty-seven different lawns in the Beaverton area, at least one time, many of them from twenty to thirty years. I also put my tractor to work during the winter months by pushing snow out of the driveways of our neighbors; from three driveways up to eight different driveways.

We lived and worked in Beaverton from December 1966 until June 2001 at which time we moved to Union City, MI. When we moved to Union City my lawn mowing task followed or even preceded me, by God's plan, as I was asked by a realtor to mow some of the lawns at the property or houses that she had for sale. I also had three people call me to ask if I would mow their lawns. So I agreed.

God used one of the ladies in Union City, to teach me more about humility, kindness and respect toward others, through her generosity. This lady and her husband had a lawn that took about one hour and forty-five minutes to mow. At this time I was asking new customers to pay me $15:00 per hour, as stated earlier. So, the first two times I mowed her lawn I asked for $25:00 for the mowing. Both times, she said, 'are you sure that is enough?' And I said, 'yes, it is more than enough'. The third time after mowing and I went to ask for my 'pay' she said to me, 'you cannot mow for me that cheap'. She gave me a fifty dollar bill. Then, to my surprise, she told me that she was going to give me 'back-pay' for the first two times that I had mowed, so she gave me another fifty dollars. During the three years that I mowed for her and her husband, she often gave me extra money and by the time I quit mowing for her she was giving me $80:00 each time that I mowed. I had a hard time learning to accept her generosity, but out of this happening, God taught me that I needed to accept the kindness of others in the same way I tried to be kind. Altogether, I have mowed twelve different lawns in the Union City area before I chose to quit at the end of 2018. Lois, my wife, due to her physical problems, needs me to be close at hand now and forty years of mowing, for others, seems long enough.

6

**Teach Sunday School class; began reading Bible

Earlier I mentioned that I was doing much Bible reading. How did this reading come about? Because I was a high school teacher, the members of the Sunday School class decided that I should be asked to begin teaching the adult Sunday School class in the Beaverton United Methodist Church that we were attending. I had never done much Bible reading until then. So I thought, if I am to teach a Sunday School class I better start reading the Bible. So I did. As stated previously, my Bible reading progressed up to the amount of reading 15 chapters each and every day, along with reading and studying the Sunday School lesson. I also, by chance—*if you believe that it was chance*—began reading Charles Colson's book "Born Again". It was because of these readings that God was able to draw me to the point of Salvation.

**Lay leader talks at BUMC

After becoming a Christian and teaching the Sunday School class for several years, God led me to the next task He created and called me to do. The Pastor at the Beaverton United Methodist Church, we attended, took a job at a church in another town, so we were without a Pastor for one summer. Because of the Pastor's absence, I was asked if I would consider leading the church services for the summer or until the church found a new Pastor. I agreed. To help me become better prepared, the church asked me to attend some Lay-speaker classes. I became a

Lay-leader for the Methodist church and was therefore qualified to speak in our church and in other 'Methodist churches' if asked. As I prepared to lead our church services during that summer, each week as I studied, God would give me some Bible verses on which, to 'build' my talk. It was a good experience to learn to rely on God to reveal what He wanted me to tell His people, in our church. Let me share one example.

One of the talks was built around the following Scriptures:

Philippians 2:3–4 *do nothing out of selfish ambition or vain conceit, but in humility consider others better than yourself. Each of you should look not only to your own interests, but also to the interests of others*
I Corinthians 10:24 *nobody should seek his own good, but the good of others*
Romans 15:2 *each of us should please his neighbor for his good to build him up*

I do not remember all of the talk that I prepared for that Sunday, but I do remember one specific part. There was a farmer that attended our church and he and his wife also attended the same Sunday School class that I taught. I will call him 'Farmer Pete' rather than use his real name. I said, 'Farmer Pete, you always like to go deer hunting each year when it is hunting season and you have set up for yourself a good tree stand in the prime area of your farm. Have you thought about the Bible verses that I have spoken about and how you should apply them to yourself and to deer hunting? If someone came to you and asked if they could hunt on your property, even if you did not know them, this is what you should do. You should give them your own tree stand because they would then have the best chance of seeing a deer to shoot.' This farmer came up to me after church and said to me, 'you sure know how to step on a person's toes'.

7

Now to the modern-day parables: they are the new understandings God has given me about some of His Scriptures. You will not read these parables in the Bible, but you will read the actual Bible verses that these parables refer to.

What is a parable? Read the following definition.

a simple story used to illustrate a moral or spiritual lesson, as told by Jesus in the Gospels

[this definition is taken from Wikipedia on the internet]

I believe that God teaches individuals, that seek Him, in ways that are unique to each individual. I developed this idea, because of the things I was taught, as I read the Bible.

When you sign your driver's license do you know that you are implying that you will learn all of the laws for driving on the state roads. You will not be able to use the excuse, if stopped by a policeman, 'I did not know that was a law'.

If you consider yourself to be a Christian, are you aware that God desires you to become a better person than you were before? God says, "Be ye holy for I AM Holy" [**I Peter 1:16**] God began a good work in you when He called you to believe in Him and in His Son, Jesus Christ. He does not want you to stop with just that belief. He wants you to become a mature person, who believes all of His Word and puts It into practice in your life.

**Holy Highway Parable

What do the Sermon on the Mount and the Michigan Vehicle Code have in common? Could there be a parable with these two?

I taught Driver Education for several summers during my teaching career at Beaverton. As a teacher I <u>think/thought</u> it <u>is/was</u> necessary to prepare myself, as much as possible, with as much knowledge about a subject as I could learn. Because of this, I purchased a copy of the <u>Michigan Vehicle Code</u> and read much of it in order to teach the students more about the laws of Michigan for driving on Michigan roads. Through this experience of reading the Michigan Vehicle Code and the Bible, God was able to teach me another metaphor or parable concerning: **The Sermon on the Mount; The Holy Highway in the desert; The Michigan Vehicle Code**.

The Sermon on the Mount is found in the Bible in **Matthew**, **Chapters 5–7.**

The holy highway is referred to in the book of **Isaiah** in four different chapters. I will give two specific references as I proceed with the parable.

Isaiah 40:3 A voice of one calling: "In the desert prepare the Way of The Lord; make straight in the wilderness a highway for our God".

Isaiah 35:8–10 And a highway will be there: it will be called the Way of Holiness. The unclean will not journey on it; it will be for those who walk in that Way; wicked fools will not go about on it. No lion will be there, nor will any ferocious beast get up on it; they will not be found there. But only the redeemed will walk there, and the ransomed of The Lord will return. They will enter Zion with singing; everlasting joy will crown their heads. Gladness and joy will overtake them, and sorrow and sighing will flee away.

So these Scriptures speak of a highway in the desert at some particular time: perhaps, it was in the past for God's people as they wandered in the desert for 40 years; perhaps it was for the Israelites as God brought them back from captivity in Babylon; perhaps it will also be in the future when we will be walking on The Holy Highway leading to The Holy City. But! Could these Scriptures have a spiritual meaning for us today? As Christians, should not we, be walking in the 'ways of the Lord?'

New Testament Scriptures tell us that we must be born again of water and the Spirit in order to see and to enter the Kingdom of Heaven, which is at the end of the Holy Highway

John 3:3 & 5 *In reply Jesus declared, "I tell you the truth, unless a man is born again he cannot <u>see</u> the Kingdom of God." "I tell you the truth, unless a man is born of water and the Spirit, he cannot <u>enter</u> the Kingdom of God."*

Who are the ransomed of the Lord and how will they be made fit for the 'holy highway'?

Psalm 15:1–3 *Lord, who may dwell in your Sanctuary? Who may live on Your Holy Hill?*

He, whose walk is blameless & who does what is righteous, who speaks the truth from his heart & has no slander on his tongue, who does his neighbor no wrong & casts no slur on his fellow man: He, who does these things will never be shaken

Psalm 24:3–5 *Who may ascend the Hill of the Lord? Who may stand in His Holy Place? He, who has clean hands & a pure heart, who does not lift up his soul to an idol or swear by what is false.*

God will allow anyone who is willing to be His servant and anyone who will allow God to redeem and purify himself, to get on the Holy Highway

Psalm 34:22 *The Lord redeems His servants; no one who takes refuge in Him will be condemned*

Titus 2:13b-14 *Jesus Christ, Who gave Himself for us to redeem us from all wickedness and to purify for Himself, a people that are His very own, eager to do what is good.*

God always saves a remnant of His people and they also will be admitted onto the Highway.

Isaiah 11:16 *There will be a highway for the remnant of His people that is left from Assyria.*

Isaiah 19:23 *In that day there will be a highway from Egypt to Assyria. The Assyrians will go to Egypt and the Egyptians will go to Assyria. The Egyptians and Assyrians will worship together.*

The **Sermon on the Mount** also lists, in the **Beatitudes**, some of the types of people who will be fit for the highway: the merciful; the pure in heart; the peacemakers, etc. God gave me an interesting 'parallel' concerning the Beatitudes as they might be displayed along the Holy Highway. In the 1950's & 1960's there used to be signs along many highways that advertised Burma Shave shaving cream. These signs were spread out with a few words on each sign, that could be read as you drove by. I have four examples to show you what they were like:

The one who drives,	*When he's been drinking,*	*Depends on you,*	*To do his thinking;*	*Burma-Shave*
Thirty days,	*Hath September,*	*April, June,*	*and the Speed Offender;*	*Burma Shave*
Within this vale,	*Of toil and sin,*	*Your head grows bald,*	*But not your chin,*	*Burma-Shave*
Drinking drivers	*Nothing worse,*	*They put the quart,*	*Before the hearse*	*Burma-Shave*

Now imagine you are moving along the Holy Highway, you might see the following signs with a different end product:

Blessed are	*the poor in spirit*	*for theirs is the Kingdom of Heaven*	*'Jesus saves'*
Blessed are	*those who hunger & thirst*	*for righteousness for they will be filled*	*'Jesus saves'*

Blessed are	*the meek*	*for they will inherit the earth*	*'Jesus saves'*
Blessed are	*the peacemakers*	*for they will be called sons of God*	*'Jesus saves'*

These signs will be written, with each of the short phrases, on successive signs.

I used to think that the Beatitudes referred to different kinds of people, some, who are peacemakers, some, who are merciful etc, but I now believe that all of the Beatitudes refer to the type of character that all Christians should have. We should be peacemakers, merciful, poor in spirit, meek, pure in heart, those who mourn, those who hunger and thirst for righteousness and those who put up with persecution because of their righteousness. These should become part of our character just as the 'Fruit of the Spirit' should be exhibited in our lives: love, joy, peace, patience, kindness, goodness, faithfulness, gentleness and self-control.

According to the MI Vehicle Code there are also other signs along the highways to control traffic flow. These signs are put in groups, by color, depending upon the information on the sign: black & white; yellow; orange; red & white; blue; green; brown. These signs are to help govern and guide our driving.

To move along the Holy Highway you must learn the same types of information, but this information may not be posted on individual signs. The needed information is all found in the Bible, much of it in the Sermon on the Mount. This is why a person, who calls himself/herself a Christian, must read the Bible, daily.

The first type of signs I will discuss are the regulatory signs that are painted <u>black & white</u> and they list 'absolute' information. Since these signs are regulatory they must be obeyed. Some examples are: the speed limit signs; do not pass signs; one-way signs. Regulatory 'signs' for the Holy Highway involve the do's & dont's that are found in the Sermon on the Mount.

Matthew 5:13 *'you are the salt of the earth'*
Matthew 5:14 *'you are the light of the world'*

Matthew 5:24 '*leave your gift in front of the altar. First, go and be reconciled to your brother, then come and offer your gift.*

Matthew 5:44 '*I tell you: love your enemies and pray for those who persecute you, that you may be sons of your Father in Heaven.*

Matthew 7:13–14 '*enter through the narrow gate. For wide is the gate and broad is the road that leads to destruction, and many enter through it. But small is the gate and narrow the road that leads to life, and only a few find it.*

These are some absolutes that we must learn to apply to our lives. We do not have a choice!

To be a holy and 'perfect' Christian, we need to read the Bible to find out what is expected of us, since God says we are <u>salt and light</u>. Salt brings out the different flavors in some foods. Since we are to be salt, does that not imply that we need to influence others in a positive way, to bring out the best in them? Too much of our salt, however, may irritate some people. As light, we need to share with others what God has taught us & to set good examples of Christian behavior.

I Peter 2:12 *Live such good lives among pagans* [even among Christian brothers and sisters] *that though they accuse you of doing wrong, they may see your good deeds & glorify God on the Day He visits us.*

I Thessalonians 1:12b *Live lives worthy of God, Who calls you into His Kingdom and Glory.*

John 3:21 *Whoever lives by the Truth comes into the Light, so that it may be seen plainly that what he has done has been done through God*

Following are some of the 'do not' ideas in the Sermon:

Matthew 5:27–28 *You have heard that it was said 'do not commit adultery.' But I tell you that anyone who looks at a woman lustfully, has already committed adultery with her in his heart.*

Matthew 5:33 *You have heard that it was said to people long ago, 'do not break your oath but keep the oaths you have made to the Lord. But I tell you, 'do not swear at all;*

Matthew 7:1 *Do not judge, or you too will be judged. For in the same way you judge others, you will be judged.*

The next absolutes, are three Scriptures that would be like our Michigan one-way signs. We need to learn of these signs from the Bible as they would apply to the Holy Highway. Neither of these Scriptures are from the Sermon on the Mount, but they are relevant to the parable.

Isaiah 30:21 *Whether you turn to the right or to the left, your ears will hear a Voice behind you, saying, "this is the way, walk ye in it"*

John 14:6 *Jesus says, "I am the Way, the Truth and the Life. No one comes to the Father, but by Me".*

Proverbs 22:6 *Train up a child in the way he should go, and when he is old, he will not depart from it.* [perhaps the way in this passage may refer to Jesus Christ, Who is the Way]

Another type of sign that is along our roadways are the yellow caution signs like: school zone; stop ahead; curve signs; no passing zones.

There are also several caution/warning verses in our 'code' for the Holy Highway.

Matthew 5:22 *But I tell you, that anyone who is angry with his brother will be subject to judgment. Again, anyone who says Raca, is answerable to the Sanhedrin. But anyone who says 'you fool' will be in danger of the fire of hell.*

Matthew 6:1 *Be careful not to do your 'acts of righteousness' before men, to be seen by them. If you do, you will have no reward from your Father in Heaven.'*

Matthew 7:21 *Not everyone who says to Me, 'Lord, Lord' will enter the Kingdom of Heaven, but only he who does the will of My Father, Who is in Heaven*

There are other yellow signs, which are the triangular-shaped yield signs. These signs alert the driver to the possibility of other drivers in the vicinity and that they will have the right-of-way, if you should both meet at the same time at a junction in the road. While traveling on the Holy Highway, with other believers, there will be times of potential conflict, especially, if those persons involved, are not mature in their Christian beliefs. The following verses from the Sermon tell a mature Christian how to react and how to be ready to yield to another person.

Matthew 5:38–39 *"you have heard that it was said, 'eye for eye, and tooth for tooth'. But I tell you 'do not resist an evil person. If someone strikes you on the right cheek, turn to him, the other one also'.*

Matthew 5:40 *if someone wants to sue you and take your tunic, let him have your cloak as well.*

Matthew 5:41 *if someone forces you to go with him one mile, go with him two miles.*

Matthew 5:42 *give to the one who asks you, and do not turn away from the one who wants to borrow from you.*

One of the most disliked signs along our highways are the dreaded orange construction signs, which often cause traffic slowdowns and backups. I can only think of one teaching in the Sermon on the Mount that refers to construction. One idea compliments good construction and the other warns of poor or improper construction. These ideas are found in the wise man/foolish man story, at the end of the Sermon on the Mount.

Matthew 7:24–27 *everyone who hears these words of Mine and puts them into practice is like a wise man who built his house on the rock. The rain came down, the streams rose and the winds blew and beat against that house; yet it did not fall because it had its foundation on the Rock. But, everyone who hears these words of Mine and does not put them into practice is like a foolish man who built his house on the sand. The rain came down, the streams rose, and the winds blew and beat against that house, and it fell with a great crash.*

If you are not familiar with the Bible and this Sermon on the Mount, the previous verses and story are telling us, that we must listen to, read and learn the words of **Matthew, chapters 5, 6, 7** and then pattern our lives after the teachings in these chapters. The rock on which the wise man built his house is actually referring to Jesus Christ, Who Is The Rock as stated in:

Psalm 18:31 *For who is God besides the Lord? And who is the Rock except our God.*

I Corinthians 10:4b *for they drank from the Spiritual Rock that accompanied them and that Rock was Christ.*

II Samuel 22:32 *For Who is God besides the Lord? And Who is the Rock, except our God*

I Corinthians 3:11 *For no one can lay any foundation other than the one already laid, which is Jesus Christ.*

The last idea about the Sermon on the Mount that I want to say something about, refers to the phrase *"everyone, who hears these words of Mine and puts them into practice"* is referring to all of the words and teachings of the Sermon on the Mount. They must become part of our lives, then we will be like a wise man with our 'house' built on Christ' teachings.

I would like to conclude the discussion of the signs that are on the Highway, for a 'moment', as we look for the sign that tells us of the presence of the Holy Highway and the correct path to follow, to get onto the Highway. This sign will be <u>green</u> in color as it is an information sign; some information signs may also, be <u>blue</u> in color. The actual sign announcing the Holy Highway is found in a Bible reference I used earlier:

Isaiah 35:8 *'and a highway will be there; it will be called **the Way of Holiness'***

So once we see the **'Way of Holiness'** sign, then we must begin looking for the correct and exact entrance to get onto the Highway. The Bible verses that tell of the correct 'entrance' to the highway are found in two other books, that are not part of the Sermon on the Mount:

John & Acts.
John 10:9 *'I am the gate, whoever enters through Me will be saved'.*
John 14:6 *'I am the Way, the Truth and the Life. No one comes to the Father except through Me'.*
Acts 4:10, 12 *'it is by the name of Jesus Christ of Nazareth: Salvation is found in no one else, for there is no other name under Heaven, given to men, by which we must be saved'.*

The Sermon also has a clear teaching about the specific entrance to the Highway;

Matthew 7:13–14 '*Enter through the narrow gate. For wide is the gate and broad is the road that leads to destruction, and many enter through it. But small is the gate and narrow the road that leads to life, and only a few find it*'.

Jesus Christ is The Narrow Gate at the entrance to The Holy Highway

After passing the 'Way of Holiness' sign, there will be an entrance ramp off of the wide worldly road that we are all on, and it leads to the 'narrow gate'. We must make a choice; the entrance to the narrow gate or stay on the wide road. Read about the choices 'man' has been given in different situations. We will have the same right to choose.

Genesis 2:16–17 '*and The Lord commanded man, "you are free to eat from any tree in the Garden; but you must not eat from the tree of the knowledge of good and evil, for when you eat of it, you will surely die*".

Proverbs 8:10–11 *Choose My instruction instead of silver, knowledge rather than choice gold, for wisdom is more precious than rubies and nothing you desire can compare with Her.*

Proverbs 9:6 *leave your simple ways and you will live; walk in the way of understanding*'.

Joshua 24:15 *But, if serving the Lord seems undesirable to you, then choose for yourselves this day, whom you will serve, whether the gods your forefathers served beyond the River, or the god of the Amorites, in whose land you are living. But, as for me & my house, we will serve the Lord*

Are there outside factors that help influence us to make the right choice? Perhaps without us even knowing it, God is at work in our lives, helping us to make the right decisions.

John 6:44 *No one can come to Me unless the Father who sent Me draws him, and I will raise him up at the last day.* [Jesus spoke these words] So in some way, God draws His people to Himself. Remember, all people in the world are traveling along a 'road of life'. Somewhere along the road they are on and at some time, they will approach an entrance to the Holy Highway. At that time they will have to make the same decision, to take the broad road or narrow road. All who choose to take the narrow road will be able to get on because of the desire of God.

I Timothy 2:3–6 God our Savior, who wants all men to be saved and to come to the knowledge of the Truth. For there is one God and Mediator between God and men, the Man Jesus Christ, who gave Himself as a ransom for all men

I Timothy 4:10 that we have put our hope in the living God, Who is the Savior of all men, and especially of those who believe.

II Peter 3:9 The Lord is not slow in keeping His promise, as some understand slowness. He is patient with you, not wanting anyone to perish, but everyone to come to repentance. But, we must also remember these Scriptures:

I Samuel 16:7 Man looks at the outward appearance, but the Lord looks at the heart.

Proverbs 20:27 The lamp of the Lord searches the spirit of man; it searches out his inmost being.

In order to get onto some of our major roadways that have been designed to be toll roads, we must pay a fee for how far we travel on them. At the toll booths, for some of the worldly roads, we must get a ticket that shows our point of entrance and the time we got on and then, when we get off, we will have to pay a toll for the distance we traveled on the road. In other cases we pay a predetermined fee for a certain distance we will travel before we get off, or until we come to the next toll booth. There is also a 'toll booth' for the Holy Highway.

Even though God wants and allows all, to get onto the 'entrance' to the Highway, we all must stop at the toll booth before actually getting onto the Holy Highway. At the toll booth, we will be asked a few questions about Jesus Christ and our belief in Him. One of the questions might be, 'have you been born again?'

John 3:3, 5 Jesus replied, 'I tell you the truth, unless a man is born again, he cannot see the Kingdom of God'. 'I tell you the truth, unless a man is born of water and the Spirit, he cannot enter the Kingdom of God'.

Another question might be in reference to your life, 'have you confessed your sins?'

Romans 10:9 *if you confess with your mouth, 'Jesus is Lord', and believe in your heart that God raised Him from the dead, you will be saved.*

If we respond in a positive manner to these questions then we are assured that we are able to get onto the Holy Highway. Jesus has paid the toll fee for all who believe in Him.

John 3:16 *For God so loved the world that He gave His one and only Son, that whoever believes in Him shall not perish but have everlasting life.*

Romans 3:22–24 *This righteousness from God comes through faith in Jesus Christ to all who believe. There is no difference, for all have sinned and fall short of the glory of God, and are justified freely by His Grace through the redemption that came by Jesus Christ.*

Ephesians 2:8–9 *For it is by Grace that you have been saved, through faith-and this not from yourselves, it is the gift of God-not by works, so that no one can boast.*

So, once we believe the preceding Scriptures and have met their requirements, we are one of those who are 'fit' to travel on the Holy Highway. Read the following Scriptures that tell of other qualifications:

Isaiah 35:8,9b-10a *A highway will be there; it will be called the Way of Holiness. The unclean will not journey on it; it will be for those, who walk in that Way. but only the redeemed will walk there, and the ransomed of the Lord will return. They will enter Zion with singing, everlasting joy will crown their heads.*

Psalm 15:1–3 *Lord, who may dwell in Your sanctuary? Who may live on Your holy hill? He whose walk is blameless and who does what is righteous, who speaks the truth from his heart and has no slander on his tongue, who does his neighbor no wrong and casts no slur on his fellow man*

Psalm 24:3–4 *Who may ascend the hill of the Lord? Who may stand in His holy place? He who has clean hands and a pure heart, who does not lift up his soul to an idol or swear by what is false.*

The three preceding verses tell of the qualifications of those that are fit for the Highway and for His Kingdom. Some, who approach the toll booth will be turned away because of God knowing their heart or because they refused to confess Jesus as their Lord.

I Chronicles 28:9b *for the Lord searches every heart & understands every motive behind the thoughts.*

Proverbs 20:27 *The lamp of the Lord searches the spirit of man; it searches out his inmost being.*

I Samuel 16:7c *Man looks at the outward appearance, but, God, looks at the heart.*

There are a few Bible verses that tell us of those that are not fit to get onto, nor walk, along on the Highway. Read the following verses:

Proverbs 21:16 *A man who strays from the path of understanding comes to rest in the company of the dead.*

I Corinthians 6:9–10 *Do you not know that the wicked will not inherit the Kingdom of God? Do not be deceived: neither the sexually immoral, nor idolaters, nor adulterers, nor male prostitutes, nor homosexual offenders, nor thieves, nor the greedy, nor the drunkards, nor slanders, nor the swindlers will inherit the Kingdom of God.*

Revelation 21:27 *Nothing impure will ever enter [the Holy City], nor will anyone who does what is shameful or deceitful, but only those whose names are written in The Lamb's Book of Life.*

The purpose of getting on and traveling along the Holy Highway is to eventually get to the Holy City, the Holy Hill, Zion or God's Sanctuary, whichever term you desire to use. But, as we travel along, we must remain strong in our faith and not disobey the signs we see along the way. Otherwise, we might get to the end of the road or the end of our life and find out that we are not fit. Read carefully the following Scriptures.

Matthew 7:21–23 *Not everyone who says to Me, 'Lord, Lord' will enter the Kingdom of Heaven, but only he who does the will of My Father, Who is in Heaven. Many will say to Me on that day, 'Lord, Lord' did we not prophesy in Your name, and in your name drive out demons and perform many miracles? Then I will tell them plainly, 'I never knew you. Away from Me, you evil doers!'*

Matthew 19:23–24 then Jesus told His disciples, 'I tell you the truth, it is hard for a rich man to enter the Kingdom of Heaven. Again I tell you, it is easier for a camel to go through the eye of a needle than for a rich man to enter the Kingdom of God'.

Matthew 22:11–13 but when the King came in to see the guests, he noticed a man, there, who was not wearing wedding clothes, 'Friend', He asked, 'how did you get in here without wedding clothes?' The man was speechless. Then the King told the attendants, 'tie him hand and foot, and throw him outside, into the darkness, where there will be weeping and gnashing of teeth. For many are invited but few are chosen'.

What will the Highway be like once we get on it? One thing we can be sure of, there will always be plenty of light to see. We will not need our own light because we will have the Light of Jesus. Several Scriptures could be sighted that speak of God's light. I have chosen to use the following Scripture that refers to the Light that the Israelites had as they moved through the desert from Egypt to the Promised Land.

Exodus 13:21 By day, the Lord went ahead of them in a pillar of cloud to lead them on their way and by night, in a pillar of fire to give them light, so they could travel by day or night.

Perhaps, we will have a similar light along the Holy Highway. The following Scriptures tell us, in different ways, that God is the Light for the world.

Psalm 119:105 Your Word is a lamp unto my feet and a Light for my path.

John 8:12 when Jesus spoke again to the people, He said, 'I am the Light of the world. Whoever follows Me will never walk in darkness, but will have the Light of life'.

John 12:46 I have come into the world as a Light, so that no one who believes in Me shall stay in darkness.

I John 1:5b,7 God is Light; in Him there is no darkness at all.—if we walk in the Light, as He is in the Light, we have fellowship with one another, and the blood of Jesus, His Son, purifies us from all sin.

Revelation 21:23 The City does not need the sun or the moon to shine on It, for the Glory of God gives it light, and the Lamb is Its Lamp.

Daniel 10:5–6 *I looked up and there before me was a man dressed in linen, with a belt of finest gold around His waist. His body was like chrysolite, His face like lightning, His eyes like flaming torches, His arms and legs like the gleam of burnished bronze,—*

Now, don't all of these Scriptures tell us how bright, **God's Light** is and will be?

There are also Scriptures that tell about the light of Christians and our need to let it shine.

Matthew 5:14,16 *You are the light of the world. Let your light shine before men, that they may see your good deeds and praise your Father in Heaven*

Matthew 13:43 *Then the righteous will shine like the sun in the Kingdom of their Father.*

Proverbs 4:18 *The path of the righteous is like the first gleam of dawn, shining ever brighter till the full light of day*

Our lives in Christ, will therefore, provide some of the Light on the Holy Highway. Once we get on the Highway there are many guidelines that we need to follow in order to make satisfactory progress.

Psalm 32:8–9 *I will instruct you and teach you in the Way you should go; I will counsel you and watch over you. Do not be like the horse or the mule, which have no understanding, but must be controlled by bit & bridle or they will not come to you.*

Proverbs 4:11–12 *I guide you in the way of wisdom and lead you along straight paths. When you walk, your steps will not be hampered; when you run, you will not stumble.*

Proverbs 4:25 *Let your eyes look straight ahead, fix your gaze directly before you.*

Hebrews 12:2 *Let us fix our eyes on Jesus, the author and perfector of our faith*

Proverbs 4:26–27 *Make level paths for your feet and take only ways that are firm. Do not swerve to the right or the left; keep your foot from evil.*

I Corinthians 9:24–27 *Do you not know that in a race all the runners run, but only one gets the prize? Run in such a way as to get the prize. Everyone who competes in the games goes into strict training. They do it* to get a crown that will not last; but we do it to get a crown that will last forever. Therefore, I do not run like a man running aimlessly; I do not fight like a man beating the air. No, I beat my body and make it a slave so that after I have preached to others, I myself will not be disqualified for the prize.

Philippians 3:12–14 *Not that I have already attained all of this, or have been already made perfect, but I press on to take hold of that for which Christ Jesus took hold of me. Forgetting what is behind and straining toward what is ahead, I press on toward the goal to win the prize for which God has called me heavenward in Christ Jesus.*

We must also be careful not to look back and long to stay at some nice place we had passed.

Luke 9:61–62 *still another said, 'I will follow you, Lord; but first, let me go back and say good-bye to my family. Jesus replied, 'no one who puts his hand to the plow and looks back is fit for service in the Kingdom of God'.*

Lot and his family were told not to look back when they were told to flee from Sodom before it was destroyed and perhaps the same warning is relevant for movement along the Holy Highway.

Genesis 19:17,26 *As soon as they had brought them out, one of them said, 'Flee for your lives! Do not look back, and don't stop anywhere in the plain! Flee to the mountains or you will be swept away'. But Lot's wife looked back and she became a pillar of salt.*

Even though a few Scriptures told us to look straight ahead and fix our eyes on Jesus as our ultimate goal, it will be OK, to glance to either side of the road to see if there might be other traffic signs coming, or to see if there might be some other traveler(s) who might need some type of help. Because Jesus has concern for all kinds of needs, He will not chastise us for looking for a chance to help others, in fact He expects us to help.

Matthew 25:40 *The King will reply, 'I tell you the truth, whatever you did to one of the least of these brothers of mine, you did for Me'.*

Three examples of stories of; 'doing for others, is doing for God' are told in the Bible. In the Book of **Mark** a story is told, that while Jesus and His disciples were walking away from the city, a blind man hollered at Jesus and asked for mercy. Instead of continuing to walk, Jesus stopped and told His disciples, *'Call him'*. When the man got to Jesus, Jesus asked Bartimaeus, *'What do you want Me to do for you'*. *'I want to see,'* said the man. *'Go'* said Jesus, *'Your faith has healed you'*. [**Mark 10:46–52**]

In the Book of **Luke** a story is told of a man, who was injured and was laying along a road and two men, a priest and a Levite walked by him without helping him. A Samaritan came to the man, cleaned and bandaged his wounds, took him to an inn and told the inn keeper to care for him and that if there were any additional costs, he would pay them when he returned. [**Luke 10:30–37**]

In **Acts 3:1–10**, Peter and John were walking up to the Temple and a crippled beggar was brought to them, asking for money. Instead of passing on by the man, Peter and John stopped and told the man that they had no money to give them but they would give him something more valuable: *'In the Name of Jesus, walk!'* The man was instantly healed.

These three stories show how we must be sensitive to the Holy Spirit who wants to and will show us, where God wants to work in the lives of others, thru us, as we move along the Holy Highway.

The following three verses tell us of the attitude we must have concerning doing works for God.

Ephesians 2:10 *For we are God's workmanship, created in Christ Jesus to do good works, which God prepared in advance for us to do.*

Galatians 6:9 *Let us not become weary in doing good, for at the proper time we will reap a harvest, if we do not give up.*

Colossians 3:17 *And whatever you do, whether in word or deed, do it all in the Name of the Lord Jesus, giving thanks to God the Father through Him.*

Read the following Scriptures that tell of what Jesus calls the 'real work of God'.

John 4:32,34 *Jesus said to the disciples, "I have food to eat that you know nothing about. My food is to do the Will of Him Who sent Me & to finish His work."*

John 5:17 Jesus said to them, "My Father is always at His Work to this very day and I too, am working."

John 6:29 Jesus answered, "The work of God is this: to believe in the One He has sent."

Getting back to some of the other signs that we will likely see along the Highway. There will be <u>blue rest area</u> signs along the way, but their wording is not found in the Sermon on the Mount.

Matthew 11:28 Come to Me, all you who are weary and heavy laden, and I will give you rest.

Hebrews 4:9–10 There remains then, a Sabbath-rest for the people of God, for anyone who enters God's rest, also rests from his own work, just as God did from His (work).

Revelation 14:13 Then I heard a voice in heaven say, 'write; blessed are the dead who die in the Lord from now on'. 'Yes', says the Spirit, 'they will rest from their labor, for their deeds will follow them'.

At these rest areas we will find places to eat that have some of the best food that you will ever taste and eat. In fact, the Sermon on the Mount tells us that some of the meals will be already prepared for us.

Matthew 6:31,33 do not worry saying, 'What shall we eat? What shall we drink? What shall we wear? But seek first His Kingdom and His righteousness, and all these things will be given you as well.'

The preceding Scripture refers to the physical food that God will provide. The next Scriptures refer to Spiritual food. The first verse even says this food is FREE. I believe the other verses also speak of free food.

Isaiah 55:1–2 Come all you who are thirsty, come to the waters; and you who have no money, come, buy and eat. Come, buy wine and milk, without money and without cost.

John 6:35 Then Jesus declared, 'I am the Bread of Life. He who comes to Me will never go hungry, and he who believes in Me will never be thirsty'.

John 6:51 *I am the Living Bread that came down from Heaven. If a man eats of this bread, he will live forever. This Bread is My flesh, which I will give for the life of the world.*

John 6:53–56 *I tell you the Truth, unless you eat the flesh of the Son of Man & drink His blood, you have no life in you. Whoever eats My flesh & drinks My blood has eternal life and I will raise him up at the Last Day. For My flesh is real food & My blood is real drink. Whoever eats My flesh and drinks My blood remains in Me and I in him.*

At these rest areas, we are also told of a perfect place to spend a night or several nights.

At the end of the Holy Highway, we will find the ultimate of ultimate, luxurious Mansion, with all kinds of rooms: banquet rooms, lodging rooms, perhaps, meeting rooms. It is called The Holy City.

John 14:2 *In My Father's House are many rooms (mansions); if it were not so I would have told you. I am going there to prepare a place for you.*

Revelation 21:2–3 *I saw The Holy City, the New Jerusalem, coming down out of Heaven from God, prepared as a Bride, beautifully dressed for her Husband. And I heard a loud Voice from The Throne saying, 'Now The Dwelling of God is with men and He will live with them. They will be His people and God, Himself will be with them and be their God.'*

8

How about the ideas of 'being born again' and the pollination of a flower? Could a modern day parable be construed from these two ideas? I think so and I will explain.

This parable came to me, in an unusual way, while I was driving the car, south, on M 99 from Lansing, MI to Eaton Rapids, MI. I was going there to attend a weekend retreat at the Eaton Rapids campground. I don't remember the exact year, but it was in the early 1980's. The thoughts started coming so rapidly and excitedly, that I had to stop the car and open up my notebook and write down the ideas before I forgot them. I wrote for a few minutes then I put my pen down, but I left my notebook open. Shortly after resuming my trip, the Holy Spirit began again, to give me new ideas. Rather than stopping the car, I started writing down notes <u>as I was driving</u>. I would look at the notebook, just for a second or two to put my pen on a new line, then I would attempt to write while watching the road. These revelations continued for several miles as I wrote a total of three pages of notes while continuing to drive.

[*I wish I had kept my original notes to see how sloppy the writing must have been.*]

This revelation that I was given, was comparing how being 'born again' is similar, to how a flower is pollinated. Both events can lead to the development of a new seed or seeds. In a plant, pollination leads to the development of new seeds, in kind and number, to those of that specific species of plants. When a person is 'born again' this leads to the development of a new 'imperishable seed' within that person which can germinate and grow into an individual who will have eternal life.

This is the summation of the pollination parable. Let us now go back to the beginning. I have written the ideas in their order of revelation. Perhaps from a purely literary standpoint the ideas could be better arranged in the eyes of some people, but, I tried to remain true to the Holy Spirit and His working in my mind. The Holy Spirit teaches us all things related to God, His ways and His thoughts. His ways and thoughts are so far above our ways and thoughts that we can only begin to understand them, if the Holy Spirit gives us the understanding. The following Scriptures bear out these statements.

Isaiah 55:8–9 *For My thoughts are not your thoughts, neither are My ways your ways, declares the Lord. As the Heavens are higher than the earth, so are My ways higher than yours and My thoughts[higher] than your thoughts.*

I Corinthians 2:11b *In the same way no one knows the thoughts of God except the Spirit of God.*

I Corinthians 2:13 *This is what we speak, not in words taught us by human wisdom, but in words taught by the Holy Spirit, expressing spiritual truths in spiritual words.*

The development of a seed begins by the process of pollination. Pollination is the transfer of pollen from the male parts of a flower; the stamen and the anther, to the female parts of a flower; the stigma and pistil.

Parts of a Flower / Stigma / Style / Pistil / Petal / Anther / Stamen / Filament / Ovary / Ovule / Stem / Sepal

Our pollination process begins when we come to the realization that we are sinners and that we must ask Jesus to come into our hearts. God, events in our lives and people around us, have all, in some way made us aware of our sin condition and we are drawn to the point of confessing our sins and asking Jesus to be our Lord & Savior.

Romans 3:23 *for all have sinned and fall short of the glory of God*
Romans 10:9 *That if you confess with your mouth "Jesus is Lord" and believe in your heart that God raised Him from the dead, you will be saved.*

God, in His own way prepares us to accept His Son as our Savior so that we can be 'born again'.

John 14:6 *I Am the Way, the Truth & the Life. No one comes to the Father, except through Me.*
John 6:44 *Jesus says, "No one comes to Me unless The Father who sent Me, draws him, and I will raise him up at the last day.*

During pollination, pollen grains are transferred from an anther to the top of the pistil, the stigma. A pollen grain is a microscopic structure that carries two sets of DNA that are necessary for the development of a seed. It also contains a third set of DNA that controls all of the actions of the entire pollen grain.

The Godhead—Father, Son and Holy Spirit—serves as our pollen for human pollination. God the Father is our whole pollen grain and the single set of DNA that controls all of our activity. Jesus Christ and the Holy Spirit are the two sets of DNA that come into each individual when they are 'born again'. All three come to each person and do the work that enables a person to become a new creature in Christ; a new creation.

II Corinthian 5:17 *Therefore, if anyone is in Christ, he is a new creation; the old has gone, the new has come.*

[The following Scriptures tell us of the 'trinity' of the Godhead.]

John 10:30 *I and The Father are One* [These are the words of Jesus]
John 14:20 *On that day you will realize that I am in My Father and you are in Me and I am in you.*
John 14:26 *But the Counselor, The Holy Spirit, whom The Father will send in My Name will teach you all things and will remind you of everything I have said to you.*

John 15:26a *When the Counselor comes, Whom I will send to you from the Father, the Spirit of Truth, Who goes out from the Father, He will testify about Me;*

As stated earlier, the pistil is the female part of a flower. It is divided into three parts: the stigma, at the top which traps pollen grains during pollination; the neck, or style which is packed with cells to limit the type of pollen tube that can grow down through it; the ovary, which is the bottom and which becomes the actual fruit, in which seeds develop.

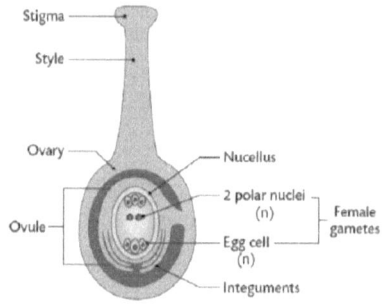

The world in which we live and the people around us make up our pistil. We must be careful that the world around us does not make us become dry and hard to the influences of God, as He tries to draw us to Himself.

II Timothy 4:3–5 *For the time will come when men will not put up with sound doctrine. Instead, to suit their own desires, they will gather around them a great number of teachers to say what their itching ears want to hear. But you, keep your head in all situations; endure hardship, do the work of an evangelist, discharge all the duties of your ministry.*

Our style, which allows things to come into our minds and hearts, is our eyes and ears, our friends, people we associate with, things we read and watch, and the worldly things and ideas around us. All of the preceding, influence our receptiveness to the things of God. If we are led too far from God and His ways, our stigma will dry up and we will not be ready for God's touch and our pollination. Somehow God

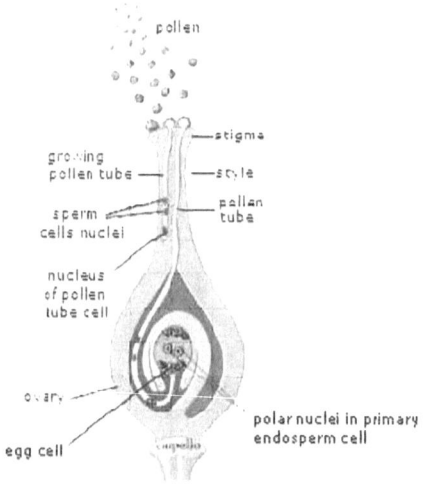

protects His own, who are only strangers in this world and He comes to them and penetrates their stiff necks and hard hearts.

John 17:14–15 *I have given them Your Word and the world has hated them for they are not of this world any more than I am of the world. My prayer is not that You take them out of the world but that You protect them from the evil one.*
I Peter 2:11 *Dear friends, I urge you as aliens and strangers in the world, to abstain from sinful desires which war against your soul.*

After pollination, the pollen grain grows a pollen tube that releases enzymes to digest the cells of the style. As the cells are digested the pollen tube continues to grow down through the style in order to reach the ovules in the ovary, at the bottom. Each type of pollen secretes an enzyme, specific to its own kind: rose to rose, corn to corn, oak to oak etc. There may be different types of pollen on the plant stigma, but, only the pollen with the correct kind of enzyme can grow down through that style. This way the ovules are protected from any wrong DNA types.

We also have to have our worldly nature and ways broken down, 'digested', so that we can recognize the things of God and become ready to receive Him. Only God has the 'correct enzymes'[*His Word, His knowledge & His Holy Spirit*] to perform our breakdown. He knows us, and what is needed to soften our hearts and prepare us for Salvation. His Word has all the teachings to destroy our immature, worldly ideas, which are worthless compared to what God has to offer. God knows our hearts and our thoughts and that they need to be changed.

Psalm 94:11 *The Lord knows the thoughts of man: He knows they are futile.*
Psalm 44:21—*He knows the secrets of the heart*
Matthew 9:4 *Knowing their thoughts, Jesus said, "Why do you entertain evil thoughts in your hearts?"*
Hebrews 4:12 *The Word of God is living and active. Sharper than any double-edged sword. It penetrates even to dividing soul and spirit, joints and marrow: It judges the thoughts and attitudes of the heart.*

We must let God tear down any worldly ways that may keep us from Him or keep Him from us. If we allow Him, God will 'eat through' our style of worldly thoughts and ways to reach our heart's door. All we have to do then, is open the door, slightly and Jesus will come in.

Revelation 3:20 *Here I am! I stand at the door and knock. If anyone hears My voice and opens the door, I will come in and eat with him and he with Me.*

Hebrews 3:12 *See to it brothers, that none of you has a sinful unbelieving heart that turns away from the living God.*

Inside the flower pistil are structures called ovules that become seeds after double fertilization. The ovule contains two different sets of DNA, the egg nucleus and the polar nuclei. Each of these sets of DNA must receive another set of DNA from the pollen tube in order for a seed to develop. During pollination the pollen tube enters a small micropyle pore of the ovule and deposits its two sets of DNA.

After the egg cell is fertilized, as it receives its new DNA, it will grow into a new embryo plant within the ovule. When the polar nuclei are fertilized and receive their 3rd DNA, they will develop

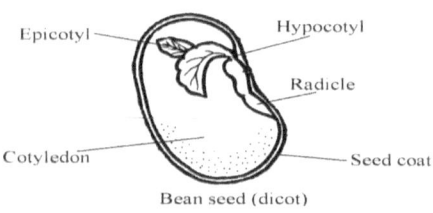

Bean seed (dicot)

into a food reserve inside the ovule to feed the new embryo plant when it is time for it to begin its new growth. Once both of these fertilizations have occurred and the embryo plant and food reserve have developed, a new seed has been made.

As unbelievers, non-Christians, we are like the ovule. We have our own DNA which needs to be fertilized. Perhaps we can liken our hearts and minds to the egg cell nucleus and we can liken our spirit or soul to the polar nuclei. Once we ask Jesus into our hearts, we must let His DNA become dominant, so that He can shape our new character. Jesus' 'DNA' in us, will make us into a new creature, a new creation.

John 3:5 *Jesus answered, "I tell you the truth, unless a man is born of water and The Spirit, he cannot enter The Kingdom of God."*

II Corinthians 5:17 *Therefore, if anyone is in Christ, he is a new creation. The old has gone, the new has come.*

Ephesians 4:24 *and to put on your new self created to be like God in true righteousness and holiness.*

Colossians 3:10 *and have put on the new self, which is being renewed in knowledge in the Image of its Creator*

I Peter 1:23 *for you have been born again not of perishable seed, but of imperishable, through the living and enduring Word of God.*

We also get a 2nd set of DNA when we are baptized with The Holy Spirit. Yes, we are a Christian once Jesus entered our heart and yes, The Holy Spirit came in at the same time. But, until we are baptized with The Holy Spirit and with fire, we usually don't allow Him to do much inside of us. He has not yet developed that reserve of His Power inside of us. He is like our polar nuclei and food reserve. The use of food gives us power. In order for us to grow and mature, we must allow The Holy Spirit to come alive in us so that He can interpret God's Word to us and make It applicable to our lives. The embryo plant cannot grow without feeding on the food reserve in the seed, neither can we grow without The Holy Spirit 'feeding' us, the meanings of God's Word.

John 14:26 *But The Counselor, The Holy Spirit, Whom The Father will send in My Name, will teach you all things and will remind you of everything I have said to you.*

I Corinthians 2:11 *For who among men knows the thoughts of a man except the man's spirit within him? In the same way, no one knows the thoughts of God except the Spirit of God.*

I Corinthians 2:13 *This is what we speak, not in words taught us by human wisdom, but in words taught by The Spirit, expressing spiritual truths in spiritual words.*

Jesus is our spiritual food upon Whom, we must feed. Jesus is The Bread of Life. He is The Word of Life made flesh. As we read God's Word, The Bible, we are feeding on The Bread of Life and the Holy Spirit interprets the words, God wants each of us to know and understand.

John 1:1–2 *In the beginning was The Word and The Word was with God and The Word was God. He was with God in the beginning.*

John 1:14 *The Word became flesh and lived for awhile among us.*

John 6:35 *Jesus declared, "I am The Bread of Life. He who comes to Me will never go hungry, and he, who believes in Me will never be thirsty".*

John 6:51 *I am The Living Bread that came down from Heaven. If a man eats of this Bread, he will live forever. This Bread is My flesh, which I will give for the life of the world.*

As we continue to feed on God's Word and allow the Holy Spirit to make it applicable to us, our character will then be molded and shaped into the image of Christ. Our old external shell, 'seed coat' is still present, but we are becoming new in mind and spirit. We still inhabit the same body, but we are inwardly being changed and renewed.

Galatians 2:20 *I have been crucified with Christ and I no longer live, but Christ lives in me. The life I live in the body, I live by faith in The Son of God, Who loved me and gave His life for me.*

[*The following was not part of my original revelation from God.*]

There are two kinds of flowering plants; annual & perennial. The annual plants only live during the season in which they are planted. Even though they produce seeds, the seeds must be planted the next year for this annual plant to continue growing as a species.

Perennial plants can grow for many successive years, in two ways; one way in which they continually grow is from their roots or tubers that stay dormant in the ground during the winter, then their reproductive cells can begin to grow a new plant when the ground and air temperatures become favorable for that plant species. The second way for new growth is through the seeds that they produced in their flowers. These seeds can fall from the plant and begin to grow the same year or they may lay dormant through the winter, then begin to grow in the spring as the weather conditions become conducive to new growth.

The problem with both of these ways of growing is that the new plant that will be produced still has DNA that is similar to its parent plant; therefore many of its characteristics will be similar to those of the parent.

The same would be true of us. We cannot be like a perennial plant. We must have new DNA put into us in order for us to become new creatures in Christ. We do not have the ability to change ourselves. Only God, through His Holy Spirit, can effect a real change in a person, after the person invites Jesus into his life and allows the Holy Spirit to live within, and to effect the changes that need to be made. [*This is the end of the added material*]

After fertilization, most seeds do not begin to grow immediately. They have to go through a period of dormancy to allow time for the embryo plant and the food reserve to develop and mature. Then the environmental conditions must be right for the seed to germinate and grow.

As a new creature in Christ, we also need time to mature before we can start living and working as a Christian. Even Jesus had to go through a period of dormancy, in the desert, 'to mature', before starting His Ministry. This was even after being baptized by The Holy Spirit.

Luke 3:21–22 When all of the people were being baptized, Jesus was baptized too. And as He was praying, Heaven was opened and the Holy Spirit descended on Him in bodily form like a dove. And a voice came from Heaven: You are My Son, Whom I love; with You, I am well pleased.

Luke 4:1 Jesus, full of The Holy Spirit, returned from the Jordan and was led by The Spirit in the desert, where for 40 days He was tempted by the devil.

Luke 4:14 Jesus returned to Galilee in the Power of The Spirit, and news about Him spread throughout the whole countryside.

During this period of dormancy, the new Christian needs to feed on the Word of God, regularly. He/she must allow the Holy Spirit to interpret what is read, so that enough understanding can occur to permit growth. As the new Christian feeds on The Word and matures he/she can begin to understand the meanings of the words, 'die to self 'and 'put on the new self'. We can then say that we are allowing the DNA of Christ to shape our inner nature to become more like Him. We will no longer consider ourselves to be number 1, nor number 2, nor number 3 etc, but rather we will consider ourselves to be at the end of the line; with God first, others second, third, etc. and us last.

Philippians 2:3–4 Do nothing out of selfish ambition or vain conceit, but in humility consider others better than yourself. Each of you should look not only to your own interests, but also to the interests of others.

Mark 9:35 Sitting down, Jesus called the Twelve and said, "If anyone wants to be first, he must be the very last and the servant of all.

Once a seed is planted in the ground, the seed coat must be porous to water, so that it can be softened to allow the embryo plant to break through, once it begins to grow. The embryo plant feeds on the food reserve in the seed, for early growth, until it develops new roots and new leaves, then it can begin to make its own food. A new Christian needs to feed on the parts of the Bible that tell who Jesus is and why He came to earth and he/she needs to 'drink' of the Living Water [*the Holy Spirit*] that Jesus will give to all who are thirsty.

John 4:10 Jesus answered her[a Samaritan woman] "If you knew the gift of God and Who it is that asks you for a drink, you would have asked Him and He would have given you 'Living Water'."

John 7:37–39 Jesus stood and said in a loud voice, "If anyone is thirsty, let Him come to Me and drink. Whoever believes in Me, as Scripture has said, 'streams of Living Water' will flow from within him." By this, He meant the Holy Spirit, whom those who believed in Him, were later to receive.

New Christians also need to learn about repentance and confession, baptism and about the love that Jesus has for all believers. New Christians should not be forced to grow too rapidly, but should be encouraged to grow at their own pace.

I Peter 2:2 Like newborn babies, crave pure spiritual milk, so that you may grow up in your Salvation, now that you have tasted that The Lord is good.

I Corinthians 3:1–3 Brothers, I could not address you as spiritual but as worldly—mere infants in Christ. I gave you spiritual milk, not solid food, for you were not yet ready for it. Indeed, you are still not ready. You are still worldly. For since there is jealousy and quarreling among you, are you not worldly?

After the embryo plant has sprouted from its old seed coat and put down its own root(s), it leaves the old coat behind as it grows a new stem and new leaf cells. As it continues to grow, new secondary leaves, larger stem cells and even new flower buds begin to develop. With all of its new parts it can produce new fruits and new seeds, that may be better, than the old, due to new DNA combinations [like hybrids].

After an initial period of apparent dormancy, while feeding on God's Word, which is our spiritual food, we must use that food to grow into new, changed and mature Christians. We must allow Christ to remold us and remake us more like Him. We need to leave our old character behind. We can do this by relying on The power of the Holy Spirit.

Colossians 3:1–2 *Since then, you have been raised with Christ, set your hearts on things above, where Christ is seated at the right hand of God. Set your minds on things above, not on earthly things.*

Romans 12:2 *Do not conform any longer to the pattern of this world, but be transformed by the renewing of your mind. Then you will be able to test and approve what God's will is, His good, pleasing and perfect will.*

Romans 13:14 *Rather, clothe yourself with the Lord Jesus Christ, and do not think about how to gratify the desires of your sinful nature.*

To allow Christ's nature and will to dominate and shape our own will, we must continue to feed on the 'food' of God that comes from the True Vine. Jesus is The Vine, and He will feed us with His Word, as long as we stay in Him. The food from The Vine will begin to fill us and begin to cause the Fruit of The Spirit to develop in us.

John 15:1 *I am the true Vine and My Father is the Gardner.*

John 15:5 *I am the Vine; you are the branches. If a man remains in Me and I am in him, he will bear much fruit: apart from Me you can do nothing.*

Galatians 5:22–23 *But the Fruit of the Spirit is love, joy, peace, patience, kindness, goodness, faithfulness, gentleness and self-control. Against such things there is no law.*

God wants the Fruit of the Holy Spirit to become the fruit of our character so we will become more like Him. He also wants us to go and produce fruit for Him, by going to 'the lost' and telling them of God's Love and the Gospel Message. If we don't produce fruit after feeding from His Vine; He gives us a warning from His Word.

John 15:2 He cuts off every branch in Me that bears no fruit, while every branch that does bear fruit, He trims clean so that it will bear even more fruit.

Luke 3:9 The axe is already at the root of the trees, and every tree that does not produce good fruit will be cut down and thrown into the fire.

Matthew 21:19 Seeing a fig tree by the road, He went up to it but found nothing on it except leaves. Then He said to it, "May you never bear fruit again." Immediately the tree withered.

Just as a new plant develops from a seed and it then produces new fruits and seeds year after year, we as Christians can live year after year and for eternity because we have been 'born again' of Jesus Christ, Who is the Imperishable Seed. Because He lives forever, we will also live forever.

Galatians 3:16 The promises were spoken to Abraham and to his Seed. The Scripture does not say, 'and to his seeds', meaning many people, but to your Seed, meaning one person, Who is Christ.

I Peter 1:23 For you have been born again, not of perishable seed, but of imperishable, through the living and enduring Word of God.

I Corinthians 15:42–44 So it will be with the resurrection of the dead. The body that is sown is perishable, it is raised imperishable; it is sown in dishonor, it is raised in glory; it is sown in weakness, it is raised in power; it is sown a natural body, it is raised a spiritual body.

I Corinthians 15:53 For the perishable must clothe itself with the imperishable, and the mortal with immortality.

9

**Raspberry Parable

In the previous chapter, I wrote about God's way of giving me a Biological analogy of pollination and being 'born again'. God used my work in the garden, at an early age, to give me another revelation, of how He can work in the life of a person. Because of our large family we always planted a large garden to grow most of the vegetables that we would eat. At that time, I did not like working in the garden for the amount of time that it took. But after maturing, I am really glad that I learned the value of work, outside, in a garden where things grow.

One day, I was standing out at our raspberry patch, holding the hose and watering the raspberry plants. As I looked at the plants and the berries, I noticed how small and dry the berries looked. I wondered if this water I was giving them, would help and how much water would I have to let soak into the ground to cause the raspberries to grow and become bigger or more plump. Suddenly, these thoughts started coming into my mind: watering the raspberry plants would allow them to develop their fruit into large, plump, juicy berries just as the Holy Spirit can cause His 'fruit' to develop in us, if we drink of His 'Living Water'. He will enable His 'fruit of the Spirit' to grow and ripen within us. His fruit is told to us in the book of **Galatians chapter 5**: the fruit of the Spirit is love, joy, peace, patience, kindness, goodness, faithfulness, gentleness and self-control. Not only will these fruits develop in us, Jesus says and promises, "If we drink of the 'Living Water' the Holy Spirit, we will never be thirsty, again". He even promises that streams of 'living water' will flow from us and perhaps influence other people.

In the 4th and 7th chapters of the **Book of John**, Jesus tells us about the Holy Spirit being the Living Water. In the 4th chapter Jesus is talking to a woman at a well. In the 7th chapter He is talking to the crowd at a feast, that day.

John 4:10 *If you knew the gift of God and Who it was that asks you for a drink, you would have asked Him and He would have given you Living Water.*

John 4:13–14 *Everyone who drinks this water will be thirsty again, but whoever drinks the water I give him will never thirst. Indeed, the water I give him will become in him a spring of water welling up to eternal life.*

John 7:37–39 *On the last and greatest day of the feast, Jesus stood and said in a loud voice, "If a man is thirsty, let him come to Me and drink. Whoever believes in Me as the Scripture has said, streams of Living Water will flow from within him". By this He meant the Holy Spirit, who those who believed in Him were to later receive. Up to that time the Spirit had not been given, since Jesus had not yet been glorified.*

As we drink of this Living Water, He, the Holy Spirit, will begin to 'soak' into our minds and 'soften' our hearts towards the things of God. Then, we can continue to grow and mature in our understandings of God and His ways. The previous Scriptures tell us that the Holy Spirit is the Living Water. But what is the ultimate source of this Living Water?

In the books of **Ezekiel** and **Revelation** we are told of a great river that flows from the Throne of God. The book of **Ezekiel** gives more details about this river than does the book of **Revelation**. Ezekiel says, in his vision, he saw water coming down from the Temple in heaven and it flowed out from under the threshold, and as it flowed, the water got wider and deeper until it became a great river.

As he walked along the river, the man who was leading him, measured the depth of the river until it got too deep to measure. The river became so deep that no one could cross.

In **Revelation**, John says that he saw the River in his vision, flowing from the Throne of God. Since this River flows from the Throne of God it will also flow from the Temple of God because God's Throne is in the Temple. Also since the River of Life comes from God and the Holy Spirit is part of the Godhead, then the Holy Spirit is part of the River of Life, called the Living Water.

Revelation 22:1–2 *Then the angel showed me the river of the water of life, as clear as crystal, flowing from the Throne of God and of the Lamb, down the middle of the great street of the city. On each side of the river stood the Tree of Life, bearing twelve crops of fruit, yielding its fruit every month. And the leaves of the tree are for the healing of the nations.*

Ezekiel 47:1–2 *The man brought me back to the entrance to the temple, and I saw water coming out from under the threshold of the temple toward the east [for the temple faced east]. The water was coming down from the south side of the temple, south of the altar. He then brought me out through the north gate and led me around the outside to the outer gate facing east, and the water was flowing from the south side.*

[I will not quote verses 3–11 that tell how big the River becomes.]

Ezekiel 47:12 *Fruit trees of all kinds will grow on the banks of the river. Their leaves will not wither, nor will their fruit fail. Every month they will bear, because the water from the Sanctuary flows to them. Their fruit will serve for food and their leaves for healing.*

How are we related spiritually, to the raspberry plants, I mentioned previously? In the 15th chapter of the book of **John,** we are told that we are the branches and Christ is the Vine. We can do nothing if we disconnect from the Vine. It is while connected to the Vine that we can get the Living Water. Plants and vines have roots that grow into the ground and it is through their roots that plants can take in water. The water is absorbed from the ground, transported through the cells of the roots and stems, and then some water is also transported into the fruit, so it can grow.

John 15:1 *I am the True Vine and My Father is the Gardener.*

John 15:4 *Remain in Me and I will remain in you. No branch can bear fruit by itself: it must remain in the vine. Neither can you bear fruit unless you remain in Me.*

John 15:5 *I am the Vine, you are the branches. If a man remains in Me and I in him, he will bear much fruit, apart from Me, you can do nothing.*

Since Jesus is our vine and since He is God, His roots grow deeply into the 'ground' of the Kingdom. In that Kingdom is the River of the Water of Life, as written about earlier, with trees planted along both sides. Jesus, as our Vine, draws water from the River of Life and as long as we are attached to Jesus, the Vine, we also get some of His Living Water. This Living Water will then, cause His fruit to begin to grow and ripen in us. We will be, 'becoming like Him'. The <u>love of God</u> will begin growing in us so that we will have the capacity to love others. The <u>joy of the Lord</u> will also be developed in us and this joy will be evident to those around us. As stated earlier, streams of living water will flow from us and these streams may be manifested through us, as we develop love for others and as we become filled with the joy of the Lord.

This was the end of my revelation concerning the watering of raspberry plants and fruit development. But I would like to add a few more ideas based on other related Scriptures. The first two Scriptures give us great hope of good things to come if we stay attached to The Vine and near its water source.

Psalm 1:1 & 3 *Blessed is the man who does not walk in the counsel of the wicked. He is like a tree planted by the streams of water, which yields its fruit in season and whose leaves do not wither.*

Jeremiah 17:7–8 *But blessed is the man who trusts in the Lord, whose confidence is in Him. He will be like a tree planted by the water, that sends out its roots by the stream, it does not fear when heat comes; its leaves are always green. It has no worries in a year of drought; and it never fails to bear fruit.*

So, when we are planted securely by 'streams of Living Water' through the reading of God's Word and as we remain attached to the Vine, then we are assured that we will grow and bear fruit, the 'good fruit' of His Spirit. The fruit that we are to bear is the 'fruit of the Spirit', as listed in **Galatians 5:22–23** *the Fruit of the Spirit is: love; joy; peace; patience; kindness; goodness; faithfulness; gentleness; and self-control*

1 Corinthians 3:6–7 *I planted the seed, Apollos watered it, but God made it grow. So neither he who plants nor he who waters is anything, but only God who makes things grow.*

John 15:16 *You did not choose me but I chose you to go and bear fruit— fruit that will last. Then the Father will give you whatever you ask in My Name.*

We are also to go and bear fruit by going to <u>the lost</u> [those, who have not accepted Jesus Christ as their Savior] and tell them about Christ's love and Salvation. We are also warned what will happen to us if we don't grow and bear fruit.

Luke 13:6–9 *Then He told them this parable; "A man had a fig tree, planted in his vineyard, and he went to look for fruit on it, but did not find any. So he said to the man who took care of the vineyard, 'For three years now, I have been coming to look for fruit on this fig tree and haven't found any. Cut it down! Why should it use up soil? 'Sir', the man replied, 'leave it alone for one more year, and I will dig around it and fertilize it. If it bears fruit next year, fine! If not, then cut it down.*

10

**Potato Hill Parable

Another parable that I was given, one day, while working in the garden involved the potatoes in a potato hill and the individuals in a church. I call this the 'potato hill parable'. This parable has Scripture that is also related to the 15th chapter of the book of **John**.

John 15:1–2, 4–5 I am The True Vine and My Father is The Gardener. He cuts off every branch in Me that bears no fruit, while every branch that does bear fruit, He trims clean so that it will be even more fruitful. Remain in Me and I will remain in you. No branch can bear fruit by itself; it must remain in the vine. Neither can you bear fruit, unless you remain in Me. I am The Vine, you are the branches. If a man remains in Me and I in him, he will bear much fruit; apart from Me, you can do nothing.

A potato plant in the garden is like the vine of **John chapter 15**. Most of this parable involves only observations that I have made as I see people in one church manifesting the same human characteristics and mannerisms as seen in the people of another church. People are the same, all over the country. I have seen the same principle involved in my teaching career. Each year or term I get new students, but I can see the same characteristics and behavior in the new students that I saw in the previous ones: 'only the names and bodies have been changed'.

When a potato plant grows, it sends out runners, like roots, that spread out in all directions and these runners go down to different depths in the soil. Most stay within 4–6 inches of the surface of the ground, if there is enough moisture in the soil. These runners are actually modified underground stems and the potatoes that grow from them are called tubers. They have the ability to make 'eyes' which are actually reproductive buds that only grow from stems. Roots can branch, like stems do, but they never develop growth buds.

As the potato plant grows it makes its own food and the excess food that it makes is transported through the stems to areas where the tuber will develop. As the food accumulates in these areas, the area swells as it fills with food and we call this swollen tuber, a potato. If you have ever dug potatoes, you know that the potatoes from one plant can be found in an area of the ground that may spread over 2 feet in diameter. The potatoes are not all, in one small area. You have to dig around in the area of the hill and you have to dig to different depths, if you want to get all of the potatoes.

Here is the parable. Some potatoes are found near the surface of the ground and are usually partially uncovered. The part that is exposed usually turns green due to the energy from the sun and the green part has a chemical that can be toxic to some people. I think this chemical is some type of acid.

In most churches, there are usually a couple of people that want to be seen by everybody. These people would be like the superficial green potatoes, that are easily seen, but they may have an 'offensive nature' about them. They are often the first people to greet you, at the door, but quickly turn away to talk to someone else that they want to impress. They also want to be on many different committees that are involved in some publicly seen activity. They might be called the 'busybodies' of the church. They often offend others by their actions. They are Christians connected to the same plant as all the other potatoes, but they have not grown and matured properly, because they have not gone 'deeply' into their study of the Bible, so that they could feed on the 'meat' of God's Word. Jesus Christ is the 'spiritual food' we must feed on to grow properly.

John 1:1–2 *In the beginning was The Word. The Word was with God and The Word was God. He was with God in the beginning*

John 6:51 *I am The Living Bread that came down from Heaven. If a man eats of this Bread, he will live forever.*

Attached to the potato plant are also some small potatoes that are in different stages of filling. These potatoes are like the new Christians in a church. They have just begun to feed on the Word of God but have not fed long enough to show much growth. But, they have been feeding on the 'real food' because they are attached to the same plant as all other potatoes. They are listening to the same preacher and are reading the same Bible.

John 15:4 *Remain in Me and I will remain in you. No branch can bear fruit by itself; it must remain in the vine. Neither can you bear fruit unless you remain in Me. I am The Vine, you are the branches.* [words of Jesus]

As you dig into the ground, at the center of the plant you will find most of the good potatoes. These potatoes have all grown to about the same size, they all have a nice smooth 'skin' or peeling and the shape of most is similar, but there is enough variance to tell one from another. These potatoes represent most of the members of the church. They have been coming to church long enough to know that they must listen to the preacher and that they must read the Bible, regularly, in order to grow properly. They have fed on the 'food from the Vine'
[*the Word of God*] long enough to have the energy and food reserves to do most of the work in the church.

Once in a while, as you dig around the potato hill, you will uncover a rotten potato. For some reason, even though it was attached to the same plant, something from the outside got into it and caused it to rot. It could have been some type of bacterial cell, some type of virus or most likely, some type of mold.

In the case of a person in the church, we know that the rotten influence could be Satan. Satan tries to see which Christian might be vulnerable to his influence; *'he sneaks around like a roaring lion, seeking whom he may devour'*. This would be like the person who started coming to church to see what was 'going on', but he never found anything that interested him, he seldom listened to the pastor nor understood him and he never read the Bible. So, when bad things began to happen to him, he had no roots with which to draw spiritual food, so he fell away.

The last type of potato that you may find in the hill is often one of the best. Often, I have uncovered the largest and best looking potato[s] around the periphery of the hill, farther out than I had expected. I had almost given up digging, thinking I had found all of the potatoes, but the thought came to dig a little wider. Most of the time I would find at least one large potato, sometimes 2 or 3, kind of 'hiding' around the periphery of the hill.

These potatoes are like the quiet, mature Christians in the church, who come faithfully every Sunday and every Wednesday night: they read and study the Bible regularly, they even ask the Holy Spirit to interpret the meaning of the Bible to them. They are waiting to be uncovered and discovered by the church leaders and waiting to be asked to fill a role in the church. For some reason, they are people that keep to themselves, until asked. Once they get involved they have much 'food' to offer because they have fed deeply, on the 'food' from the Vine and the Bible. These mature Christians are like the wise man at the end of the 'Sermon on the Mount' in the books of Matthew and Luke, who dug down deep and set the foundation of their houses, their beliefs, on the solid Rock, Jesus Christ.

All of the potatoes are connected to the same plant and they get the water that is needed from the same bunches of roots and they all get the same type of food that is made by the plant. In the Scripture reference, listed earlier, Jesus says that He is the Vine and His Father is the Gardner.

In **1ˢᵗ Corinthians chapter 3 verses 6–8,** the Bible says, *that one person plants the seeds or the plants, and another person waters them, but it is God, Who makes them grow.* So it is with us as we feed on God's Word by reading the Bible, by attending a Sunday School class or by listening to preachers that preach God's Word. These help us get the information but it is God, through His Holy Spirit, Who gives us the understanding. He makes the Truth of His Word grow in our minds and in our hearts.

11

**Church Potluck Parable

How many of you reading this book attend church regularly and also enjoy eating at the church potlucks that your church provides? [I hope you have church potlucks] Well, the next parable that I have in this book discusses how a church potluck and reading the Bible should affect us, in a similar manner.

Ez 3:1–4 *And He [God] said to me, "Son of man, eat what is before you, eat this scroll; then go and speak to the houses of Israel." So I opened my mouth and He gave me the scroll to eat. Then He said to me, "Son of man, eat this scroll I am giving you and fill your stomach with it." So, I ate it and it tasted as sweet as honey in my mouth. He then said to me, "Son of man, go now to the house of Israel and speak My words to them."*

Rev 10:8–11 *Then the voice that I had heard from Heaven, spoke to me once more, "Go, take the scroll that lies open in the hand of the angel, who is standing on the sea and on the land." So I went to the angel and asked him to give me the little scroll. He said to me, "Take it and eat it. It will turn your stomach sour, but in your mouth, it will be as sweet as honey." I took the little scroll from the angel's hand and ate it. It tasted as sweet as honey in my mouth, but when I had eaten it, my stomach turned sour.*

In the Scriptures listed above, God is telling the prophet Ezekiel that he should take the scroll that God has in His hand and eat it. In the Revelation scripture, a Voice is telling the apostle John, to take the scroll from the angel's hand and eat it. Both of these scriptures speak of eating a scroll, which also has the Words of God, just as the Bible has.

The 6th chapter of the Gospel of John tells about Jesus feeding the 5000 and later in the chapter it says, that He is the 'Bread of Life' that came down from Heaven. As I was reading this chapter, one day, the thoughts started coming to me that we need to feed on 'This Bread', just as we would eat at a church potluck. And we feed on 'This Bread' as we read the Word of God.

Jesus is the Word of God, made flesh, and we learn this idea from the Book of John. These are the first few verses of the book of John.

John 1:1–2 *In the beginning was the Word, and the Word was with God and the Word was God. He was with God in the beginning.*

John 1:14 *The Word became flesh and lived for a while among us. We have seen His glory, the glory of the One and only Son, Who came from the Father, full of grace and truth.*

God became flesh through the person of Jesus Christ. The Word became flesh when Jesus became flesh. Therefore, Jesus is the one referred to when Scripture says that the Word became flesh and dwelt among men. Jesus is also called: the Bread of Heaven; the Bread of God; the Bread of Life; and the Living Bread, that came down from Heaven, upon Whom, we must feed.

John 6:32 *Jesus said to them, "I tell you the Truth, it is not Moses, who has given you the bread from Heaven, but it is My Father, Who gives you the True Bread from Heaven."*

John 6:33 *For the bread of God is He who comes down from Heaven and gives life to the world.*

John 6:35 *Then Jesus declared; I am the Bread of Life. He who comes to me will never go hungry, and he who believes in Me will never be thirsty.*

John 6:51 *I am The Living Bread that came down from Heaven. If a man eats of This Bread, he will never die. This Bread is My flesh, which I will give for the life of the world.*

[Jesus said the preceding words to the Jews and to a crowd of followers]

At a church potluck, there is always a lot of food, more, than can usually be eaten by those present. So when the announcement is made about the potluck, the announcing person usually says that everyone should stay and eat, even if you did not bring a dish to pass, because there will be plenty of food. Usually there are leftovers.

God invites all to come to Him to be part of His Family, just as all are invited to the church potluck.

I Timothy 2:1, 3–4 *I urge, then, first of all, that requests, intercession and thanksgiving be made for everyone. This is good and pleases God our Savior, who wants all men to be saved and to come to a knowledge of the Truth.*

Matthew 22:1–2, 9–10 *Jesus spoke to them in parables, saying, "The kingdom of Heaven is like a king, who prepared a wedding banquet for his son. He sent his servants [and said] 'Go to the street corners and invite to the banquet, anyone you find.'" So the servants went out into the streets and gathered all the people they could find, both good and bad, and the wedding hall was filled with guests.*

John 10:16 *I have other sheep that are not of this sheep pen. I must bring them also. They too, will listen to My Voice and there shall be one Flock and One Shepherd.*

John 11:51–52 *As high priest that year [Caiaphas] prophesied that Jesus would die for the Jewish nation and not only for that nation, but also for the scattered children of God, to bring them together and make them one.*

Revelation 5:9b *With Your blood, You purchased men for God from every tribe, and language and people and nation.*

Even though all are invited to attend the potluck and invited into the Kingdom of Heaven, not all choose to attend. Many think there are other things that are more important.

Matthew 22:3, 5 *Jesus sent His servants to those, who had been invited to the banquet to tell them to come, but, some of those invited refused to come; others paid no attention and went off—one to his field, another to his business.*

For all of those, who come to the wedding banquet, there is also a warning in this parable.

Matthew 22:11–14 *But when the king came in to see the guests, he noticed a man there, who was not wearing wedding clothes. "Friend," he asked, "how did you get in here without wedding clothes?" Then the king told the attendants, "Tie him hand & foot & throw him into the darkness, where there will be weeping and gnashing of teeth. For many are invited, but few are chosen."*

Matthew 7 has still another warning to all, who are invited:

Matthew 7:21 *Not everyone who says to Me, 'Lord, Lord', will enter the Kingdom of Heaven, but only he who does the will of My Father, Who is in Heaven.*

What are the Wedding Clothes for the Banquet?

Revelation 19:7–8 *For the Wedding of The Lamb has come & the Bride has made Herself ready. Fine linen, bright & clean was given Her to wear.*

[Fine linen stands for the righteous acts of the saints]

Matthew 5:20 *For I tell you, that unless your righteousness surpasses that of the Pharisees and the teachers of the law, you will certainly not enter the Kingdom of Heaven.*

Isaiah 64:6 *All of us have become like one, who is unclean and all our righteous acts are like filthy rags.*

Romans 1:17 *For, in the Gospel, a righteousness from God is revealed, a righteousness that is by faith, from first to last, just as it is written, 'the righteous shall live by faith.'*

Romans 8:10 *But, if Christ is in you, your body is dead because of sin, yet, your spirit is alive because of righteousness.*

I Corinthians 1:30 *It is because of Him that you are in Christ Jesus, Who has become, for us, Wisdom from God—that is, our righteousness, holiness and redemption.*

In preparation for the potluck, the food is brought in and placed on the counter[s], the drinks are prepared, the tables are set and arranged neatly so that people can move around between them, then the people are asked to find a place and sit down and get ready for someone to say a blessing for the food.

When Jesus fed the 5000, He made similar types of preparations. He asked His disciple, Philip, "Where shall we buy bread for these people to eat?" Andrew, another disciple said, "We have found a boy who has some bread and fish." So Jesus told the disciples to have the people sit down and get ready and then He would say a blessing.

John 6:9 *Here is a boy with 5 small barley loaves and two small fish, but how far will they go among so many?*

John 6:10–11 *Jesus said, "Have the people sit down". There was plenty of grass in that place and the men sat down, about 5000 of them. Jesus then took the loaves, gave thanks, and distributed to those who were seated as much as they wanted. He did the same with the fish.*

In **Luke,** the Scripture says that He even told the disciples to have the crowd sit down in groups.

Luke 9:14 *He said to His disciples, "Have them sit down in groups of about fifty, each."*

As people are getting ready to sit down for the potluck, many will look around and try to decide which table will be told that they can go first, so that is where many try to sit. But, we have to be careful with these kinds of thoughts. We should rather be willing to sit at the table that will go last and allow others to go ahead of us.

Mark 9:35 *Jesus called the Twelve and said, "If anyone wants to be first, he must be the very last and a servant of all.*

Luke 14:10–11 *But when you are invited,* (to a banquet) *take the lowest place, so that when your host comes, he will say to you, 'Friend, move up to a better place.' Then you will be honored in the presence of all your fellow guests. For everyone who exalts himself will be humbled and he who humbles himself will be exalted.*

Proverbs 25:6–7 *Do not exalt yourself in the king's presence and do not claim a place among great men; it is better for him to say, 'Come up here,' than for him to humiliate you before a nobleman.*

At the potluck there are all kinds of food set out before us on the tables. We get to choose which types of food we want to eat. If you are like me, you will usually take some type of leafy salad, some type of jello salad, some meat, vegetables, and potatoes. We first choose to take the kinds of food that we like best, then if there is room on our plates, we may even try to put our favorite type of desert on our plate, before it is all taken.

We may even try some other type of food that looks good. This choosing of food is like reading only the best known parts of the Bible; like only reading the:

'Sermon on the Mount', _Matthew 5,6,7;_ the 23rd Psalm; the Love chapter of _I Corinthians 13_; and perhaps the 'faith' chapter found in _Hebrews 11_. This type of reading is incomplete.

We must learn to feed on the whole Word of God.

Deuteronomy 8:3 _Man does not live on bread, alone, but, on every Word that comes from the mouth of the Lord._

II Timothy 3:16 _All Scripture is God-breathed and is useful for teaching, rebuking, correcting and training in righteousness, so that the man of God may be thoroughly equipped for every good work._

Romans 15:4 _For everything that was written in the past, was written to teach us, so that, through endurance and encouragement of the Scriptures, we might have hope._

Many people attend each of the potlucks that a church has in order to enjoy all of the different types of foods that are brought. No one could feed on all of the kinds of food at a potluck at one time. There would not be enough room in their stomach to hold all of the food. Neither can anyone sit down to read the whole Bible, at one time, and be able to take it all in. God has enough 'food' in His Word, for all to eat and there will always be more than can be eaten, at any one time. We need to develop a habit of regular Bible reading, where we study a few chapters at a time or where we study related topics from different chapters. In this way we can begin to get an understanding of all of God's Word.

Acts 17:11 _Now the Bereans were of more noble character than the Thessalonians, for they received the message with great eagerness and examined the Scriptures every day to see if what Paul said was true._

II Timothy 2:15 Study, to show thyself approved unto God, a workman, that needeth not be ashamed, who correctly handles the Word of God

After the meal is over, the cleanup must take place and the leftover food must be taken care of. Jesus told the disciples to take care of the left-overs after He fed the 5000.

John 6:12–13 When they all had enough to eat, He said to His disciples, "Gather the pieces that are left over. Let nothing be wasted." So they gathered them and filled 12 baskets with the pieces of the 5 barley loaves left over by those who had eaten.
Matthew 15:37 They all ate and were satisfied. Afterward, the disciples picked up 7 basketfuls of broken pieces left over [feeding of the 4000]

The last idea about the potluck refers to what many people do after they get home. Their stomachs are so full that all they want to do is sit down and do nothing, except take a nap. When we have fed on God's Word, the Bread of Life, we must put that knowledge to work. We cannot take in His Knowledge, then do nothing with it.

James 1:23 Do not merely listen to the Word, and so deceive yourselves. Do what it says.
James 2:17 In the same way, faith by itself, if it is not accompanied by actions, is dead.

So we must put our food and faith into action and begin to work. One time, when Jesus' disciples told Him to eat something; Jesus replied, *'I have food to eat that you know nothing about. My food is to do the will of Him Who sent Me and to finish His work'. John 4:32& 34.*

So, we must have the same attitude. We must not come to church only to enjoy the potlucks, but we must come to church to feed on the Word of God, that we hear in a Sunday School class and that we hear from the pastor during his sermon. Then we must go home and develop a time of daily feeding on God's Word, so His Word can prepare us to do 'His Work'.

Our work must be the kind of work that God, The Father is always doing. Jesus tells us that we must not work, just for food that will spoil.

John 6:27 *Do not work for food that spoils, but for food that endures to eternal life, which the Son of Man will give you.*

What is the 'work of God'? The following Scriptures should lead us into a fuller understanding of His work.

John 4:32 *But, He[Jesus] said to them, "I have 'food' to eat that you know nothing about."*

John 4:34 *"My food," said Jesus, "is to do the will of Him, Who sent Me and to finish His work."*

John 5:17 *Jesus said to them, "My Father is always at His work, to this very day and I, too, am working."*

John 5:36 *"I have testimony weightier than that of John. For the very work that the Father has given Me to finish and which I am doing, testifies that the Father has sent Me.*

John 6:27 *"Do not work for food that spoils, but for food that endures to eternal life, which the Son of Man will give you."*

John 6:29 *Jesus said, "The work of God is this: to believe in the One, He has sent."*

John 9:4 *"As long as it is day, we must do the work of Him, Who sent Me. Night is coming, when no one can work."*

I used to be confused about the Scripture that says that God is always at His work, because in ***Genesis 2:2*** the Bible says that on the 7th day of creation, He finished His work, then He rested. I finally realized that the Genesis Scripture is only talking about resting from His 'creation workings'.

So even though God rested on the 7th day, after His creating of the universe, He is always at His work of trying to bring people to believe in His Son, the Lord Jesus Christ, Whom He sent to be the Savior of all who would believe [***John 3:16***]. We must learn to join the Trinity in Their work of Salvation. We must learn to go to God, in prayer, asking Him, what He wants us to do for Him, and to whom, is He wanting to send us.

These are the five new modern day parables that God revealed to me as I read and studied the Bible for many years. As you do the same with your Bible(s), my hope is that God will reveal to you what He wants to teach you and in ways that are unique to you. I also hope that

God will use some idea(s) in this book to draw you to Him, if you have not yet been drawn.

John 14:6 *I am the Way, the Truth and the Life. No one comes to the Father except through Me.*

John 6:44 *No one can come to Me unless the Father, Who sent Me, draws him and I will raise him up at the Last Day*

12

*****Memorized 33 Bible verses while mowing lawns for others

I wanted to start this new chapter, with an attention grabbing idea. As I read the Bible I asked God, what do the Scriptures I memorized mean and how do they apply to my life? How must I change my life to live what the Scriptures really mean? The Bible verses that I committed to memory all refer to how a person should live, if he/she calls him/herself a Christian. Most of the verses are found in the books of Ephesians, Philippians and Colossians.

In order to memorize the Bible verses while mowing, I did the following. I actually got out three-by-five cards and wrote down the 33 Bible verses, one on each card. Then I took a hole punch and punched a hole in the top left corner of each card. I then got a large snap ring and put all of the cards on the ring, which was large enough to go around the steering column of my riding lawn mower. As I was mowing I would look at one card, read the verse and then repeat it over and over until I had committed it to memory. I would then go to the next card and do the same thing. I did this day after day while mowing lawns for the twenty to thirty people that I mowed for. Memorizing these Bible verses and meditating on them has helped me to try to put them into practice in my life. Through these Scriptures, God has helped me understand how my life must change so that I would be living in the way these Scriptures tell me/us to live?

The following are some of the verses that I memorized.

Ephesians 2:10 *[for] we are God's workmanship, created in Christ Jesus, to do good works, which God created in advance for us to do*

Galalations 6:9 *Let us not become weary in doing good, for at the proper time we will reap a harvest, if we do not give up*

I Corinthians 15:58b *always give yourselves fully to the work of the Lord, because you know that your labor in the Lord is not in vain*

Colossians 3:17 *[and] whatever you do whether in word or deed, do it all in the Name of The Lord Jesus, giving thanks unto God, thru Him*

Philipians 4:13 *I can do all things through Christ who strengthens me*

II Thessalonians 3:13 *And as for you, brothers, never tire of doing what is right*

Romans 12:1–2 *offer your bodies as living sacrifices, holy & pleasing to God—which is your spiritual worship. Do not conform any longer to the pattern of this world, but be ye transformed by the renewing of your minds. Then you will be able to test & approve what God's will is; His good, pleasing & perfect will*

Ephesians 4:29 *do not let any unwholesome talk come out of your mouth, but only what is helpful in building others up, that it may benefit those who listen*

Philippians 2:3–4 *do nothing out of selfish ambition or vain conceit, but in humility consider others better than yourself. Each of you should look not only to your own interests, but also to the interests of others*

I Corinthians 10:24 *nobody should seek his own good, but the good of others*

Romans 15:2 *each of us should please his neighbor for his good to build him up*

Romans 12:18 *if it is possible, as far as it depends on you, live at peace with everyone*

I Thessalonians 5:15 *Make sure that nobody pays back wrong for wrong, but always try to be kind to each other and to everyone else*

Hebrews 12:14 *make every effort to live at peace with all men and to be holy; without holiness no one will see God*

I Peter 1:16 *be holy, because I am holy*

Psalm 139: 23–24 *Search me, O God, and know my heart, test me & know my anxious thoughts. See if there is any offensive way in me and lead me in the way, everlasting.*

Psalm 51:10–11 *Create in me a pure heart, O God, and renew a steadfast spirit within me; do not cast me from Your presence, nor take Your Holy Spirit from me.*

Psalm 26:2 *Test me, O Lord, and try me, examine my heart and my mind*

Psalm 119:11 *I have hidden Your Word in my heart, that I might not sin against You.*

Along with God giving me the five modern day parables, the Commencement address that I have written in the first part of this book and the memory verses, He has also enabled me to develop a concordance of His Word. Here is what I mean.

During the times I have been reading the Bible, I have written down many words that seemed to 'stand out' in a particular Scripture verse, then I would think, I have read a similar verse that has the same word. So I would hunt up the other verse that had the same word then I would write down both Scripture references. Here is an example: <u>teacher</u>: Matthew 12:38 / Mark 9:38 / Luke 10:25. These verses, along with 36 others, each tell of someone referring to Jesus as a teacher or they are addressing Him as a teacher.

Another way that I took notes was to write down a Scripture reference then write down other references of related Scriptures. The following Scriptures are one example:

Ephesians 2:10/ Galations 6:9/ I Corinthians 15:58 Each of these Scriptures refer to Christians as being created by God, to do good works for Him, by helping others.

Every blank page in my old and first NIV Bible is filled with words and Scripture references that I wrote as notes for myself. I am using all of these notes to form my own concordance. My computer shows me that I have actually typed 337 pages of Scriptures in the format of a concordance.

As a teacher I learned to take many notes so that I could teach my students about Biology and God has shown me how to take notes in concordance form, so He could teach me about Himself. Here is one short example:

JESUS KNEW:

John 16:19 *Jesus 'saw' that they wanted to ask Him about this,—*

Jo 6:61 Aware that His disciples were grumbling about this, Jesus said to them,—

Jo 6:64 "Yet there are some of you, who do not believe." For Jesus knew, from the Beginning, which of them did not believe & who would betray Him.

Jo 18:4 Jesus, knowing all that was going to happen to Him, went out & asked them—

As I continue with this writing, I will give different examples of how I am putting various Scripture verses into a concordance. These are the verses that have become meaningful to me. I will use a key word and put it in bold type to begin each section of related Scriptures. I will also write a short explanation of how these Scriptures have become meaningful to me.

BIBLE STUDY:

II Timothy 2:15 *Do your best to present yourself to God as one approved, a workman who does not need to be ashamed and who correctly handles the Word of Truth*

I wonder if God 'led me' to put the above verse into practice without me even knowing the meaning of this verse. I taught high school Biology in Beaverton High School for 34 years. In order to prepare myself to become a teacher, I purchased five different copies of the textbook that I would be using. Each night, I would read through the whole chapter that I would be talking about the next day, in order to make my lecture notes. I would then read the same chapter in all five texts that I had, to see if there might be other ideas to add to my notes. I was also afraid and felt intimated, that I would not know the answers to the questions, that my students would or might ask. I did this amount of reading every school night for the first three years I taught. Finally, I came to realize that I may never know the answers to any or all of the questions that I might be asked. I learned to tell the students, 'I don't know the answer, but I will try to find the answer, with your help'. I also taught Human Anatomy for eleven years in two different two-year colleges. So I had a teaching career of forty-five years.

Referring back to the 'workman' verse listed above, I also used those ideas to prepare myself for teaching a Sunday school class. Many years ago, I was asked to teach the Sunday school class that my wife and I were attending at the Beaverton United Methodist Church. As a high school teacher, I knew the importance of knowing the material that I was to teach. Because of this background, I knew that I must begin reading the Bible, if I wanted to teach a Sunday school class. Even though I had been raised in a family that went to church every Sunday, I was never encouraged to read the Bible nor do I remember seeing my mom or dad reading the Bible. I did not become aware of the real meaning of the workman Bible verse, until after much Bible reading. In both my teaching and in my Bible study, I believe that I put the meaning of this verse into practice without even realizing I was doing it. God gave me the desire to read His Word and to study the Biology books so that I would become an approved workman for Him, in both teaching endeavors.

The following three verses have also become very important to me as a teacher. God's call for me was to become a teacher, so these Scriptures tell me that I must do the best job that I can. I must know the subject matter good enough to give the correct explanation and to be able to answer the questions that I would be asked. I kept these Scriptures in mind while preparing to teach Biology and while preparing to teach the things about the Bible to the Sunday School class.

Romans 12:6, 7 We have different gifts—If it is serving, let him serve; if it is teaching let him teach;
James 3:1 Not many of you should presume to be teachers, my brothers, because you know, that we, who teach will be judged more strictly.
Titus 2:7–8 In your teaching, show integrity, seriousness & soundness of speech that cannot be condemned, so that those who oppose you may be ashamed, because they have nothing bad to say about us.

DEEPER UNDERSTANDING:
John 14:6 Jesus says, "I Am the Way the Truth and the Life. No one comes to the Father, but by Me"

During my readings and studies of the Bible, I have developed an idea about the preceding Scripture that is different from most interpretations. This is a well known Scripture, but might it have a deeper meaning than most people understand? Most Bible scholars, teachers and preachers tell us to be careful and not to take Scripture verses out of context. They must be interpreted within their context. But, could there be a deeper meaning in this Scripture, that only God can reveal to a person, in a way that would be unique to that person? Let me explain.

Most leaders of in a church say that each child/person has his/her own way in which they should be brought up. I agree. But, can there be a different and deeper understanding of *John 14:6*?

My new thought about this verse is as follows; if a parent would train-up their child in, The Way, the Truth and the Life of Jesus Christ, when that child grows up, he will not depart from that way, 'The Way'. As a workman, who has been trained by reading God's Word regularly, I believe that my new idea can be an acceptable handling of this verse. I base my thoughts on the following Scriptures.

Proverbs 22:6 *Train a child in the way he should go and when he is old, he will not turn from it*

Psalm 86:11 *Teach me Your Way O Lord and I will walk in Your Truth; give me an undivided heart, that I may fear Your Name*

Ephesian 6:4 *Fathers, do not exasperate you children; instead, bring them up in the training and instruction of the Lord*

John 10:27 *My sheep listen to My voice; I know them and they follow Me*

I believe that my idea is a deeper understanding of what God wants us to know about how to bring up our children. We need to bring our children up in a loving and Christian home. Perhaps we should be reading some Bible verses to them along with some children's Bible stories. We should also be taking them to Sunday school, when they are young, so they can hear others tell them children's Bible stories. This will set a precedence for them, that church attendance is important. These are a few ways to bring up our children in the Way of God.

ONE TEACHER:

Matthew 23:1, 10 *Then Jesus said to the crowds & to His disciples: "Nor are you to be called teacher, because you have One Teacher, The Christ."*

John 13:13–14a *'you call Me **Teacher** and Lord, and rightly so, for that is what **I Am**. Now that I your Lord and **Teacher**'* —

After reading thru the Bible, several times, I began thinking, that thru-out the story, of God leading His people, that He spoke to them, in only one way at a time; He used 'One Teacher' at a time: In the beginning, God talked directly to various people as He told them what He expected of them & what He wanted them to do: He spoke directly to, Adam & Eve; Abraham & Sarah; Moses & Aaron: then He used Moses & Aaron to speak to His people, Israel; then He used the major prophets; then the minor prophets; then John the Baptist, who preceded & prepared the way for Jesus; then Jesus talked directly to God's people & to all who would listen; then Jesus sent the Holy Spirit. The Holy Spirit is now the 'Voice of God', that God uses to teach all who ask for His Wisdom. If we do not ask the Holy Spirit the meanings of the Scriptures we read, we will only get a partial understanding of them. But, we must remember that The Holy Spirit will only tell us the meaning of a Scripture(s) that He wants to reveal, to us, at a particular time. He knows what we need at any one time. We probably would not be able to understand all of the meanings of God's Word, if it was given to us at one time. We must learn to ask The Holy Spirit to teach us all things related to God & related to God's Word. Without the Holy Spirit revealing God's thoughts to us, we can only get a superficial understanding of the actual meanings of the Scriptures.

The following Scriptures are some of the key Scriptures, that I have found, that tell of the Holy Spirit's teaching, those who ask.

John 14:26 *But the Counselor, the Holy Spirit, Whom the father will send in My Name, will teach you all things & will remind you of everything I have said to you.*

John 16:13 *But when He, the Spirit of Truth, comes, He will guide you into all Truth. He will not speak on His Own; He will speak only, what He hears & He will tell you what is yet to come.*

I Corinthians 1:17 *For Christ did not send me to baptize, but to preach the Gospel; not with words of human wisdom, lest the Cross of Christ be emptied of Its Power.*

I Corinthians 2:4 *My message & my preaching were not with wise & persuasive words, but with a demonstration of the Spirit's Power, so that your faith might not rest on men's wisdom but on God's Power.*

I Corinthians 2:11b *No one knows the Thoughts of God except the Spirit of God.*

I Corinthians 2:13 *This is what we speak, not in words taught us by human wisdom but in words taught by the Spirit, expressing Spiritual Truths in Spiritual Words*

13

CAREFUL WORDS:

Remember, that I told you, that way back in the 1950s, God told me that someday <u>I would be a coach</u>. He did not say what kind of a coach I would become.

I would like to tell of a situation in which I was confronted by a potentially harmful situation. I had been hired by Beaverton High School as a Biology teacher, with the understanding that I would also be given a coaching job when a position opened. I was given a job as an assistant coach with the two varsity football coaches. My job was mainly as a trainer to take care of the injuries to the varsity players. I did no real coaching. The third year in my career, I was given the varsity basketball coaching job, because the school board took the job away from the current varsity coach. Little did I know that the same thing would happen to me, three years later. Some of us teachers were sitting in the teacher's lounge, at lunch one day, when in walked this man who said,

"Hi, my name is Larry Niederstadt, and I am the new varsity basketball coach". At the time of this writing, I have still not been told officially, 'by the school' why they took the job from me. **BUT!!**

I actually had a good coaching career for twenty-two years. But, it did not start until I made peace with God, so that He could make peace in my heart towards the Beaverton School Board for taking away the varsity basketball coaching job from me. For the remainder of that year I was really upset and mad at the school board for taking the coaching job from me and not telling me, it was going to happen. Every day for the rest of the year I kept hoping I could walk into the school board room and slap down my letter of resignation and walk out. But I was unable to find another teaching job in other school districts, even though I had interviews at four different schools. Even though I was quite upset, I never said any words that were hurtful or reckless towards the people I came in contact with, even with those in administration.

Ephesians 4:29 *do not let any unwholesome talk come out of your mouth, but only what is helpful in building others up, that it may benefit those who listen*

Proverbs 12:18 *Reckless words pierce like a sword, but the tongue of the wise brings healing*

A Christian must always be careful about the way he/she talks. Our words must always be kind words and words to help others that may be hurting in some way. This would be the kind of character that God expects of His people and of those who call themselves Christians. No matter the circumstances, whether good or bad, we must be careful of the words that we use. It is usually easy to think of kind words to use in good situations and when talking to people that we know and like. But, when exposed or confronted by unkindly people or their words, we may be tempted to react in ways that are similar. This is when we must 'step back' and think of the preceding Scriptures. Am I thinking of unkind, reckless or unwholesome words. This must not happen. Because of the above two Scriptures I was able to keep my emotions under control and not react recklessly with unkind and hurtful words toward the school administration and the school board.

I actually coached JV Basketball, with Larry, as the varsity coach for several years. We became very good friends during our years while coaching together. My whole coaching career consisted of 3 years helping out with varsity football, 21 years as head JV football coach, 9 years varsity baseball, 2 years JV baseball, 3 years as varsity boys basketball coach, 15 years JV boys basketball,7 years JV girls basketball, 5 years girls JV volleyball, 3 years as girls varsity volleyball coach and finally 2 years as varsity boys golf coach. During my JV football coaching, the first two seasons the teams went undefeated, because of the God-given talent that the players had, then a few seasons later, the team had no wins. During my JV basketball coaching, we had one undefeated season and one season we had no wins. I found out that the longer you coach the more variety of successes and failures you will have.

MEDIOCRITY:

'Living above the level of mediocrity', what does this expression really mean? While reading the Bible everyday and trying to allow God to reveal a better understanding of His Word, He actually lifted me above reality, in my thoughts, in a couple of situations.

One day, on the opening day of school for teachers we were told to report to the cafeteria area for the start of our meetings. Most of the teachers hurried to the area trying to be first in line to sign up for various prizes that were to be handed out and to be in the front of the line to get the free doughnuts, rolls, bagels and coffee that were provided. God gave me an impression to just stand back and to look at how the people were reacting as though this was the most important thing they could do at this time. Few wanted to wait.

I had a similar experience at a church potluck. Instead of hurrying to get in line early, I felt the urge to just wait and let all the others to get in line before I did.

There will still be food to eat when I get there. If I am trying to put the following two verses into practice, then I must allow others to get in line ahead of me.

Philippians 2:3–4 *do nothing out of selfish ambition or vain conceit, but in humility consider others better than yourself. Each of you should look not only to your own interests, but also to the interests of others*
I Corinthians 10:24 *nobody should seek his own good, but the good of others*

I was at the gym at Central Michigan University in Mt Pleasant one night during a basketball tournament game. As I watched several spectators goofing around during the national anthem and during the introduction of the players, especially those from the opposing team, I wondered if they ever read the Bible, went to church or had any thoughts about God. Each time an opposing player's name was announced there would be many and loud catcalls about that name.

As I thought about these various ways in which people were reacting to worldly ways, I thought how hard it will be for them to listen to words and teachings about God. Their hearts are too far away at this particular time. Only God will know how and when to 'call them'. As a Christian I must be ready to be used by God, if asked, to help provide 'this call' to others.

14

SALVATION:

Many people may memorize various Bible verses, but do they take time to actually think about the verses and what they really mean. I am not a preacher nor did I go to college and take Bible courses. I am only relating how God has made these Bible verses meaningful to me.

John 14:6 I AM the Way, the Truth and the Life. No one comes to the Father but by Me
John 6:44 No one can come to Me unless the Father, Who sent Me, draws him and I will raise him up at the Last Day

These two verses are important for becoming a Christian. Jesus Christ is the only person in whom we must believe and through Whom, Salvation is possible. Many people say that a person must be 'born again' before they can be saved, then they use the Scriptures from **John 3:3, 6** where Jesus is talking to Nicodemus. Nicodemus had asked Jesus, 'what must I do to be saved?' So Jesus answered and said, "I tell you the truth, unless a man is born again, he cannot see the kingdom of God." He also told Nicodemus, "I tell you the truth, unless a man is born of the water and the Spirit, he cannot enter the kingdom of God". Many people use these two verses as the only way for people to be saved and then they proceed to have a person repeat what they call the 'sinners prayer'. But there may be as many types of sinners prayers as there are people who say them.

I would like to suggest that there may be many ways for a person to come to believe in God and to be saved. During my years of Bible reading, I have taken many notes and organized many Scriptures into a concordance. I have used the term, Salvation, as one of the topics in the concordance. I have listed more than fifty Scripture verses that tell of being saved, twenty one verses say that a person only has to believe in the Lord Jesus Christ to be saved. If you read through all of these Scriptures you may find a common thread regarding Salvation and a person's Salvation may not be limited just to **John 3:3&6.** Read the following three Scriptures as examples of having a belief in Jesus Christ.

John 6:47 I tell you the Truth, whoever believes in Me has everlasting life.
John 11:25–26 Jesus said to her, "I am the Resurrection & the Life. He, who believes in Me will live, even though he dies; & whoever lives & believes in Me will never die."
John 12:42 Yet, at the same time, many, even among the leaders, believed in Him.

Going back to the two verses that I began with, God will draw a person to begin to seek Himself and His Son, Jesus Christ. God, in His Own way, will draw each person to Himself and to Jesus in 'the way' that God knows that person will respond to. Each person is an individual, who God created and only He knows what they need and how they will respond to 'His call', and this response will be unique to each person. Perhaps, in the story of Nicodemus, Jesus was telling him, specifically, that he needed to be born again, because Jesus knew Nicodemus' heart.

God also knows the proper time in which to begin the call to each person. I am speaking from personal experience. I had been reading the Bible for several years and was reading 15 chapters everyday, usually in the morning. All of this reading plus reading Charles Colson's book "Born Again" were the ways that God called me to become a believer. Since becoming a believer, God has shown me how to use His Word in my everyday walk of life. Allow me to share with you one way in which God helped me use His Word to help in my coaching career. I am using the following Scripture as an example.

APPLICATION:

Proverbs 3:5–6 *Trust in the Lord with all your heart, and lean not on your own understanding; in all your ways acknowledge Him and He will make your paths straight*

Earlier in this book I related the story of how my JV basketball team had a perfect 20-0 season. I used the above verse as an application of God's Word to plan for the upcoming game with the team from Evart, that would be our possible nemesis to a perfect season. God answered my prayers to Him that week by giving me two new ideas to use to prepare for the game. You can refer back to the earlier part of the book, titled the 20-0 season.

15

DO FOR OTHERS:

Another verse that became very important to my everyday life and work is the following.

James 1:27 Religion, that God our Father accepts as pure and faultless is this to look after orphans and widows in their distress and to keep oneself from being polluted by the world.

This Scripture verse became a dominate verse that guided my life and work after being done with teaching for the day. One part of God's plan for me in Beaverton, was to become a lawn mower or as I thought later, He took me to Beaverton to become a 'care-taker of God's green earth in Beaverton'.

My wife and I were blessed with twin boys and one daughter to raise as our children. When our boys were in Jr High, as 7th graders, three widow ladies in our church asked Lois and I if we would allow our boys to mow their lawns for the summer. We said, yes, we would give them permission and this was the beginning of my/our mowing for God by helping others.

After the church service was over and we got home, we asked the boys if they would want to mow the widow ladies lawns to make some money. They excitedly replied, yes! The first year the boys only had the three lawns to mow for the widow ladies. So I would take them to the lawns on

Saturday and watch them mow and help them out, if they got too tired or hot. The next year, our number of lawns to mow, expanded to eight lawns.

I bought a riding lawn mower for the boys so that they/we could get all the lawns mowed, each week. Then the third year the number of lawn customers went up to fifteen. One night, in prayer, I told God that if He would give me the ability to buy a new, bigger, riding lawn mower I would put it to work for Him, by doing for others as His Word tells us to do. Well, He did and I/we mowed for others for the next 40 years. Most of the time I/we had 22-25 lawns to mow, each week. My twin boys helped with the lawn mowing for the six years that they were in school. Most of the people that the boys and I helped were widow ladies, retired people or handicapped people. I did mow for a few neighbors and friends that we knew but, who did not fit the 'needed' category. Our pay started out by the three widow ladies agreeing to give each of the boys, $3.50 per hour. As new people asked us to mow their lawns, we told them that we would charge them $7.00 per hour, the same as the twins, were first paid. As I got new customers, I stayed with the same hourly wage after the boys left high school and no longer helped me. As the years increased and I continued mowing for the same people, they voluntarily gave me more money than I asked for. After 30 years of mowing the increase that people were giving me amounted to $15.00 per hour. Do for God and He will cause the increase.

I also used my tractor to serve God and others during the winter. I bought a snow blade and mounted it to the tractor and then used it to push the snow out of our neighbors driveways. There were seven houses from our house to the main road. When more than two inches of snow fell at one time, I would plow the snow out of all the driveways from our house to the main road. I never asked any of the neighbors for money for plowing their driveways. If they came out and offered, I accepted. But remember, earlier I told God that I would put my tractor to serving Him by serving others. So I did.

The following three verses also became very meaningful to me, so that I kept helping others. Even though my first calling from God was to be a coach, He put these verses in my mind and heart, as more important or a second calling to help others. So after 21 years of coaching several sports, I felt it to be more important to give up the coaching jobs and only help the widows and people that I mowed for.

Philipians 2:3–4 *Do nothing out of selfish ambition or vain conceit, but in humility, consider others better than yourselves. Each of you should look, not only to your own interests, but also to the interests of others*
I Corinthians 10:24 *Nobody should seek his own good, but the good of others*
Matthew 25:40 *The King will reply, "I tell you the Truth, whatever you did to one of the least of these brothers of Mine, you did for Me"*

One day while finishing up a lawn that I had mowed, I was doing the trimming around the trees and the house. As I finished and was walking back to the truck I looked around to see if I had missed anything. I saw a few blades of grass around one tree and thought, oh well, those few blades won't matter, then the words of the two Scriptures listed below, came to mind. If you are taking care of these lawns to serve God, then you have to go back and cut down those few blades of grass. You are to do the best you can and to make the lawns look the best possible, all for the glory of God. The following verses tell me what I must have in mind, while mowing for others.

Colossians 3:17, 23 *And whatever you do, whether in word or deed, do it all in the Name of the Lord Jesus, giving thanks to God the Father through Him *Whatever you do, work at it with all your heart, as working for the Lord, not men*
I Corinthian 10:31 *So whether you eat or drink, or whatever you do, do it all for the glory of the God*

16

Here are some other verses that I have applied to my life, that tell me how to think of others.

Romans 12:18 *if it is possible, as far as it depends on you, live at peace with everyone*
Romans 15:2 *each of us should please his neighbor for his good to build him up*

Have you ever thought about these two verses and how to apply them to the life you are living? The first thing that stands out to me is that all people that we come in contact with are to be considered as our neighbors. No matter where they live, they are our neighbors here on earth. Therefore we must not look down on anyone. In fact, we must look for opportunities to help as many people as we can.

One example of how I have put these verses into practice is by giving my neighbor well water. One day I was talking with my neighbor about how to grow things in a garden. She told me that she was going to try to start a few garden plants in the few small planters that she has. The lawn in the back of her house goes down quite steep, so steps were built down the slope and small planters were built along the sides of the steps. She is trying to grow a few fruits and vegetables, in these planters, but she does not want to use the city water that comes into her house. Like most cities, chlorine is added to the water to kill bacteria that may be present. So I told her that she could use water from the well that I had someone dig, when we first moved into our house.

I planted my own lawn and I wanted to grow vegetables in my garden. I did not want to use city water to water the lawn and the garden, because the water bill would go too high. So, about three times a week, she brings over several water jugs, I drag my hoses around to the front of the house and fill up her water jugs. I then volunteer to carry the five gallon pail of water over to her garage, while she and her two young daughters carry the other containers of water over. This helping becomes very pleasing to all four of us. They get the water they need and I get the benefit of helping my neighbors. With the two verses quoted from Romans, above, and the following two verses, we should be encouraged to actively seek to help others in what ever way we can.

Philippians 2:3–4 *do nothing out of selfish ambition or vain conceit, but in humility consider others better than yourself. Each of you should look not only to your own interests, but also to the interests of others*
I Corinthians 10:24 *nobody should seek his own good, but the good of others*

GOD'S WORK:
Ephesians 3:20–21 *now to Him who is able to do immeasurably more than all we ask or imagine, according to His power that is at work within us; to Him be glory in the church and in Christ Jesus throughout all generations, forever and ever*

The preceding verse says that God can do anything He wants to do and He can do more than we could ever imagine or understand. He is omnipotent. But, I would also like to suggest that He would like to do much of His work through His people, you and I, people that are Christians. We can do all the work God has planned for us to do, if we rely on the power that He has available to us through His Holy Spirit. I believe that the following Scriptures support the idea I have, that God does want to work through His people.

Ephesians 2:10 *for we are God's workmanship, created in Christ Jesus, to do good works, which God created in advance for us to do*

I Corinthians 15:58b always give yourselves fully to the work of the Lord, because you know that your labor in the Lord is not in vain

Ephesians 6:7–8 Serve wholeheartedly, as if you were serving the Lord, not men, because you know that the Lord will reward everyone for whatever good he does, whether he is slave or free

Philipians 4:13 I can do all things through Christ who strengthens me

Galations 6:9 Let us not become weary in doing good, for at the proper time we will reap a harvest, if we do not give up

There are actually two types of work that God wants done. The first I will write about is the type of work I did. I taught high school Biology for 34 years in the Beaverton High School in Beaverton, Michigan. During this same time I had many coaching assignments, as I related earlier. I did this coaching after our school hours were over, then I also had several mowing jobs to do in the evenings. It usually took me until dark to get the lawns mowed each evening that needed mowed. God gave me the desire to mow for the people and He also gave me the energy to get all of my work done. During this time of teaching, coaching and lawn mowing, I wonder how I was able to do it all. How did I have the energy and time to do it all? My only explanation is that since God called me to Beaverton to be a coach, and a teacher and to help others. He also gave me the desire and energy to accomplish His work.

The other type of work that God wants done, is His work, which is to bring people to believe in Himself. I wrote about this type of God's work in an earlier part of this book. He wants all men/people to come to a belief in Him. We, His people, are to help Him in this endeavor by living for Him and telling others. Our lives are to demonstrate our belief in God and to help others develop the same type of belief. It has been easy for me to do the physical work for others, but telling others about God, I have not been as productive. I'm hoping that the work that I have done for all of these people will demonstrate a God-like character. With some of the people I have had an opportunity to tell them why I mow for them and why I try to do the best I can, because it is to honor God.

After completing your reading, if you have any comments or questions, you may contact me through my email address: jobkerahabe24@gmail.com

www.ingramcontent.com/pod-product-compliance
Lightning Source LLC
Chambersburg PA
CBHW021004150626
46549CB00012BA/1071